ONE HUNDRED AND FIVE SONGS OF OCCUPATION FROM THE WESTERN ISLES OF SCOTLAND

THE ENGLISH FOLK DANCE AND SONG SOCIETY

The Society organises thousands of events each year, maintains a list of clubs and events of interest to members, provides a source of information on singers, dancers, mummers and events run by other organisations, supports and encourages traditional performers, runs training courses, workshops, lectures and classes, owns the unique Vaughan Williams Memorial Library, publishes a magazine, books and tapes covering all aspects of our traditions, is a registered charity, and is a trustee of Cecil Sharp House, England's National Folk Centre.

For information concerning membership, write to the:

**English Folk Dance & Song Society,
Cecil Sharp House,
2 Regent's Park Road,
London NW1 7AY.**

ONE HUNDRED AND FIVE SONGS OF OCCUPATION FROM THE WESTERN ISLES OF SCOTLAND

collected by

Frances Tolmie

Reprinted from the Journal of the Folk-Song Society., No. 16, 3rd part of vol. IV., 1911.

ISBN 1 86143 038 8

Llanerch Publishers reprint 1997.

PREFACE.

THE following collection is offered to the Folk-Song Society with considerable diffidence. It consists merely of the notes and fire-side memories of two friends, natives of the Hebrides, who are fully aware of many gaps amongst the verses; gaps which, to their regret, they are now unable to repair in the way that would be most efficient, by returning to those haunts of early youth from which they have been separated for many years.

FRANCES TOLMIE.

37, Merchiston Crescent, Edinburgh.
December, 1911.

INTRODUCTION.

MISS FRANCES TOLMIE'S collection of one hundred and five Songs of Occupation from the Western Isles of Scotland opens a mine of interest and delight to musicians, poets, folk-lorists and historians, and undoubtedly forms one of the most important contributions yet made towards the preservation of the purely traditional music and poetry of our British Isles in general and of Scotland in particular.

Songs of occupation are amongst the most primal things in the history of mankind, and in their simple rhythms and intervals, first evolved by workers for their needs, we find the germs of all Music and Verse.

The songs in this *Journal*, which represent but a small section from Miss Tolmie's mass of Gaelic memories and lore, have not only been skilfully taken down, translated and annotated by a Hebridean familiar with Highland Song from earliest infancy, but have received the valuable commentary of another Highlander, Dr. George Henderson, Lecturer on Celtic Languages and Literature in the University of Glasgow, and well known as an authority and writer on Celtic lore and literature. In addition, Miss A. G. Gilchrist, a constant student of comparative folk-song, has carefully analysed each air here printed, and has contributed to the *Journal* a very illuminating and suggestive essay upon the gapped-scale system to which these pure Gaelic tunes conform.

Patrick M'Donald, in his admirable preface to *Highland Vocal Airs* (published 1781), writes as follows: "In writing them [the tunes] out, he has endeavoured to follow, as closely as he could, the manner in which they are sung: and he has given them to the public in the same form in which he received them. Perhaps, he has not always given the best sets of them. . . . A perfect uniformity in the manner of performing vocal airs is not to be expected: more especially if they have never been written out in musical characters. . . . Hence better or worse editions or sets of the same air will be obtained from different persons, or in different parts of the country. When the publisher had frequent opportunities of hearing an air, he chose that set of it which appeared to him the best, and the most genuine. When he had not such opportunities, he satisfied himself with writing the notes which he heard." No words could better define Miss Tolmie's methods and the views which she holds as regards her own collection; but those who have themselves noted Highland songs will realise how faithfully she has preserved their characteristics in the versions here presented.

It should be borne in mind that songs of occupation as a whole belong to the *luinneag**** class, which is distinct from that of the *laoidh*, hymn or Ossianic lay,† and the *oran mór*, "great song."‡ To the latter classes belong the grand elegies and laments, songs of praise, rhapsodies descriptive of the beauties of nature and the like, in which, to suit the words, the music flows in broad and majestic streams. Patrick M'Donald writes : "Over all the Highlands, there are various songs, which are sung to airs suited to the nature of the subject. But on the western coast, benorth middle Lorn, and in all the Hebrides, *luinigs* are most in request. These are in general very short, and of a plaintive cast, analogous to their best poetry : and they are sung by the women, not only at their diversions but also during almost every kind of work, where more than one person is employed, as milking the cows, and watching the folds, fulling of cloth, grinding of grain with the quern, or hand-mill, hay-making, and cutting down corn. The men too have *iorrums*, or songs for rowing, to which they keep time with their oars, as the women likewise do in their operations, whenever their work admits of it. When the same airs are sung in their hours of relaxation, the time is marked by the motions of a napkin, which all the performers lay hold of. In singing, one person leads the band ; but in a certain part of the tune he stops to take breath, while the rest strike in and complete the air, pronouncing to it a chorus of words and syllables generally of no signification."

To the *luinneag* class, therefore, must be referred the bulk of the songs in this *Journal*, although examples of both *laoidh* and *oran mór* appear amongst them, these having been found an appropriate accompaniment to work.

The airs of these *luinneagan*, composed of primitive intervals, short phrases, strong accents and rhythms of great variety, are not only very valuable for the musical historian, but on closer acquaintance reveal a beauty, dignity, and emotional capacity unsuspected by the superficial reader.

As regards the texts of the songs, a few remarks are here offered for the sake of those to whom Gaelic life and literature may be quite unfamiliar.

From time immemorial the history and legends of the Highlands of Scotland have been preserved and transmitted orally by bards, who committed to verse and song all that seemed worthy of being remembered. Every family of distinction had its bard or bardess who acted as poetical chronicler and genealogist. Professor Magnus Maclean

---

* Usually translated "ditty," but cognate with Irish *luinnioc* = chorus, glee ; Middle Irish *luindiuc*, *luindig* = music-making, from proto-Celtic *lundo*, root *lud*, as in *laoidh*. *Cf.* English *lay*. (MacBain's *Ety. Gaelic Dicty.*)

† An old Highlander considered it becoming to take off his bonnet when reciting such. (*Sàr Obair.*)

‡ There is also the *duanag*, defined by singers as a "little song" or "ditty," a small lyric usually dealing with rural things and love.

in his *Literature of the Celts* writes: "The Highland bards before the Forty-five were thus a goodly company, and they had this in common, that they were independent for the most part of writing, in some cases even of education; yet they had a wonderful command of their native Gaelic, and an extraordinary ear for the beauties of sound that may be expressed through the medium of language. They were all more or less attached to chiefs, whose praises they sang, and almost without exception these early bards lived into extreme old age, and died in the land they had never left, and among the friends they had never forsaken."

The office of bard was in many cases hereditary. A notable instance is that of the MacVurich family which for seventeen generations furnished bards to the Clanranald branch of Macdonalds, thus acting as poets and local historians from the time of the famous Muireach Albanach (*circa* 1200), some of whose poems appear in the *Book of the Dean of Lismore*, down to the beginning of the nineteenth century, when the illiterate Lachlan MacVurich gave such interesting testimony concerning the Macdonald manuscripts in the custody of his father, amongst which was the famous "Red Book' mentioned later. As a poet Neil MacVurich, born at the beginning of the seventeenth century, seems to have been the most distinguished descendant of Muireach Albanach. Of the wonderful poetess Mary Macleod we all know, though the exact date of her birth remains still uncertain. It is asserted by various writers that the year of her birth was 1569. Dr. Henderson is doubtful concerning this, and believes that she was born about the beginning of the seventeenth century. The latter date has therefore been given throughout this *Journal.*

Besides these recognised and official bards there have always been numerous lesser bards, the Highlander's natural form of self-expression being verse and song. Hence the numberless traditional songs, old and new, that we find still in the Gaelic-speaking parts of Scotland, which, originally improvised in moments of joy, grief, indignation or amusement, have become the property of a whole country-side. I recall a satirical song of seventeen stanzas, composed by a Ross-shire man * during the absence of a laggard errand-lad and sung to the culprit on his return. Another song of no great age—also from Ross-shire—was made by a member of one respectable clan in derision of a well-known neighbouring sept. From Lewis I have songs improvised by the singer's brother to ridicule a blacksmith who had shod his horse ill, and to describe the restlessness of a working-lad who wished to be with the girl whom he loved. Yet another song in my collection was made within recent years by a poor shepherd,

---

* This poet, a crippled tailor of a generation ago, spared no one from the lash of his terrible satire, and his songs would have formed a large collection by themselves. On the occasion above referred to, he vowed that he would make a stanza a minute during the messenger's absence, and did it easily.

who, having left a larger island to settle in Pabbay, describes his hardships and melancholy solitude in poignant words.

For the Highlander of the past, oral tradition was the only means by which verse and music were preserved. To quote Patrick M'Donald once more: "Till lately such compositions were seldom committed to writing, but were handed down by tradition, from one generation to another. That works of taste and genius should be preserved without the assistance of letters, may appear somewhat incredible to us, who derive our knowledge chiefly from books. But among an illiterate sequestred people, living at their ease, the memory is amazingly tenacious, especially when the matter to be remembered coincides with the ruling passion." He adds that "love and satire, petty war and the pleasures of the chase always were the favourite themes of the Highland bards."

Formerly few Gaels could read Gaelic; fewer still could write it. And at the present day the larger proportion of Gaelic-speaking people, having acquired their general education through the medium of English (a language foreign and even unintelligible to many Highlanders still), cannot read the tongue which they habitually use. No book in the Gaelic language was printed in Scotland before 1567, when a translation of Knox's *Liturgy* was published. In the seventeenth century three books and a catechism were translated and printed in Gaelic; but until after 1745 Scotland had no printed Gaelic literature of her own. In 1767 the New Testament was printed in Gaelic, but not until 1805 did a Gaelic version of the complete Bible appear. The nineteenth century opened a period of comparative activity in the printing of Gaelic books.

With the exception of the famous MS. called the *Book of the Dean of Lismore*, consisting of Gaelic poetry taken down from oral tradition between 1512 and 1526; the *Fernaig* MS. collection, made by Duncan Macrae of Inverinate, Kintail, in Ross-shire, between 1688 and 1693; the *Book of Clanranald* (consisting of two MSS. known as the "Red" and the "Black"), and portions of a very few Gaelic MSS. in the Edinburgh Advocates' Library, there remain but small fragments of written bardic poetry of the more distant past. Certain MS. collections of Ossianic lays and other poems, made during the eighteenth century by literary Gaels (such as the Rev. Donald Macnicol of Lismore and Appin, the Rev. James Maclagan of Blair Atholl and Dr. Hector Maclean of Mull), have fortunately been preserved, as also some collections referred to by J. F. Campbell of Islay in *Leabhar Na Feinne* and by Dr. Alex. Cameron of Brodrick in *Reliquiæ Celticæ*; but too many others, made at various times, were destroyed or lost * through ignorance, carelessness or accident,

* Amongst them, the collection made by Mrs. Fraser of Giùsachan which was carried by her son, Captain Simon Fraser, when accompanying his regiment in the American War, and that made, through her aid, by the Rev. John Farquharson of Inverey, Balmoral, when missionary at Strathglass. This he took to Douay when Prefect of Studies there, and during the French Revolution it disappeared.—G. H.

before the movement for rescuing Scottish Gaelic remains began to make itself felt some fifty years ago.

In face of the foregoing facts, the interest and importance of Gaelic traditional song-texts at once become apparent. We have in them legend, history and lore which owe nothing to broadsides, chap-books or other printed matter such as has influenced the folk-song and story of countries that have for centuries had their vernacular literature. Fragmentary as the legend and history preserved in them may now be, we find, therefore, that Gaelic traditional songs put us in touch with a long and romantic past, with verse and music of an older and more untouched type than is found elsewhere in British folk-song.

From the primitive modes in which the airs are cast one must attribute to them a great age. A Highland singer usually knows nothing of the origin of the tunes which he sings, though he often knows the name of the poet, old or new, whose words he repeats, and may indeed have composed the poem himself. "There is *nothing* like these beautiful songs which are handed on from mouth to mouth; but most of all it is the beauty of the *words! There is nothing in the world* like these splendid words!" cried a singer of Loch Morar district to the writer, with passionate enthusiasm.* As a rule, Highlanders use the tunes as vehicles for their verse and are frequently almost unaware what tune they are using. Ask the singer of an original poem whether he composed the air to it and he will sometimes answer that he is not sure how much he "may have made" and how much is like something that he "may have heard somewhere." At other times he will show where he has adapted an old tune to suit his own words.

The pathetic and wild beauty of Gaelic songs can only be realised by those who have heard them sung. Highlanders are very commonly gifted with fine voices, of a rich resonance similar to that found amongst Italians. In Gaelic the vowels are open and pure, often succeeding and melting into each other as they do in Italian. Thus, very strong *messa di voce* vowel effects are produced, which heighten emotional expression in an extraordinary manner. The soft gutturals, more like those found in Dutch than in German, and the trilled R's are very vocal. Gaelic words have the strong accent on the first syllable, and in many words the last syllable is as elusive as the French mute "e" when properly sung.† This strong accent and weak ending in Gaelic words were observed, and entirely misunderstood, by Lowland-Scottish and English musicians

* The same singer said, after first seeing her songs noted, " It is a very beautiful work, the saving of these grand poems and ancient, ancient airs." One day, after singing an *oran mór*, learnt from her very old father, then living, she said "I always thought this song would die with my father Now I know that it will not be so."

† *Cf.* note by A. G. G. on p. 182.

of the late seventeenth century onwards, and it is these manufacturers of "Scottish music" who are responsible for the invention of the odious "snap" which arouses the indignation of the true Scot, if he have anything of music in him.

The Highlander makes marked use of the *crescendo* and the *diminuendo*; phrasing, more especially when moved, with very great breadth and power.

He accents vigorously, and makes much use of the *sforzando* on vowels. Generally he uses grace-notes, varying them with every verse. Some singers, chiefly the older people, ornament as over-profusely as do many of the Irish, but as a rule Gaels adorn their airs sparingly and with musical good taste. They have a peculiar and characteristic way of carrying on one musical interval to the next by means of a rapid repetition and slide of the first note, producing a beautiful and soft kind of *appoggiatura* or *portamento* (not a "scoop,") such as is heard in plain-song when skilfully recited. Very commonly the Gaelic singer beats time with his foot, or foot and hand together. An excellent analysis of the Highland manner of singing is given by Patrick M'Donald, who justly dwells upon its wild, free and expressive effect.

The songs in this *Journal* owe their existence in print to one described by a Celtic scholar as having "rare talent and exceptional knowledge of Skye and its traditions." [*] In her own words, she "did not mean to make a collection, but simply to arrest further decay in the old songs." This she has done in a way only possible to a native of the Highlands who combines wide culture with musical gifts, and who herself sings the songs as she heard them sung around her. Miss Tolmie has for years been well known to the "master-gleaners" of Gaelic lore, to whose publications she has often contributed, though usually preferring to do so anonymously. It was in her youth whilst in Edinburgh, that at the house of the late Mr. Thomas Constable Miss Tolmie first became acquainted with a large library of printed Celtic literature, and with scholars actively concerned in the preservation of Celtic tradition; and in Mr. Constable's family and social circle she received the intelligent sympathy and help which encouraged her to save from oblivion what was so familiar to herself and so beloved.

Where traditional matter is concerned all links with the past are of value, and therefore with the collector's permission a few details of interest, omitted from her "Notes and Reminiscences," are here added.

Miss Frances Tolmie is descended through both parents from Hebridean families whose homes during long centuries have been in the Western Isles of Scotland, and whose members have left honourable names behind them, as tacksmen (*i.e.* holders of land on long lease according to ancient Scottish tenure), as soldiers, doctors and

---

[*] *Survivals in Belief among the Celts*, George Henderson (MacLehose, Glasgow, 1911).

ministers living self-sacrificing lives. The name TOLMIE was until a generation ago spelt TOLME. MacBain in his *Etymological Dictionary of Proper Names* states that it is formed from the Norse *holm* (an islet), which for Gaelic-speaking purposes required a T before the H. Other old Gaelic forms are TOLM, TOLMACH and TOLMAIGH (genitive of TOLMACH). The latter is most akin to the modern name.*

According to tradition the Tolmies came from Scandinavia to the West of Scotland with the progenitors of Clan Leod (Macleods) during the great Viking invasions.

Miss Frances Tolmie's great-grandfather, William Tolme, called "Uilleam Mór" because he was so tall, went from his home at Fortrose † to live for some years in the Island of Lewis. Leaving Lewis early in the eighteenth century, he settled in Skye as "factor" (*i.e.* land-agent) to Macleod of Macleod, managing the three estates of Macleod's country in Skye, Harris and Glenelg on the Inverness mainland. At that time rents in the Western Highlands were still paid not in money but in kind. William Tolme's son and grandson (the latter being Mr. John Tolmie, the collector's father) occupied Uignish near Dunvegan, and there, in the Macleod Country of Skye, Miss Frances Tolmie was born.

The clan of MACASKILL—spelt also MACASKELL and M'CASKELL—to which Miss Tolmie's mother belonged, is also of Norse stock. The name ASKELL or ASKETIL (meaning the "ketil" or sacrificial vessel of the gods.) is found in different forms, in Icelandic poems of the tenth century, and in early records. Oscytyl was Abbot of Croyland in 992, and Askel was King of Dublin in 1159. In 1311 Gilbert Macaskel or Mackaskill was Keeper of the Isle of Man to King Edward III. The progenitor of the Skye branch of the sept fled from Ireland in consequence of a feud relating to the Norse kingship there. He came to Skye, where he was received in a friendly manner by Macleod and given lands there. During the period of hereditary jurisdiction MacAskill's descendants filled the office of Lieutenant to the Chief, and guarded the coasts against marauders. A MacAskill was also Macleod's hereditary henchman, who carried him over rivers, or through sea when landing from his galley, and was his trusty right hand by night and day. After the Forty-five, when the system of local government was changed, these offices gradually lapsed.

Miss Tolmie's maternal great-grandfather, the Rev. Malcolm MacAskill, in 1763 became the first Presbyterian minister of Eigg. His son "Eóghann Bàn" (Eoghan

---

* For very interesting information concerning the names and history of the Tolmie and MacAskill families, *see* also Mac Iver Campbell's *Account of Clan Iver*, p. 13; G. Henderson's *Norse Influence on Celtic Scotland* (J. & A. Constable, Edinburgh), p. 56, and A. W. Moore's Manx Names (*Surnames of Scandinavian Origin*), p. 51.

† Fortrose on the mainland and Stornoway in Lewis were the commercial centres of Ross-shire at the time.

the Fair-haired), the subject of a song in this *Journal*, was a striking figure and a great athlete. One day, whilst putting the stone, Eoghan threw his stone such an astonishing distance that the people of Eigg kept it where it fell and called it "the stone of Eoghan." Not many years ago, when workmen strangers to Eigg were fencing round the little meadow where the stone lay, they shifted it a short distance, whereupon the islanders raised a vigorous protest and insisted on its being restored to precisely its old position. It lies now where it fell close upon a century and a half ago.

Eoghan's brother, Donald MacAskill, grandfather to Miss Tolmie, was tacksman of Kildonan in Eigg, and doctor of the Small Isles. In the year 1817, he and the parish minister were returning late one night from Arisaig to Eigg in an open boat. Some cattle on board becoming restive, the boat suddenly capsized and the minister and doctor, encumbered by their cloaks, were drowned—Donald MacAskill in the prime of life. A fellow-passenger, a tailor, got safely to shore by clinging to a cow's tail. He was always known afterwards as "Taillear a'Mhairt" ("The Tailor of the Cow") and his family as "Clann-Taillear a'Mhairt."

Dr. Donald MacAskill's daughter, Margaret Hope MacAskill, born in 1808, married Mr. John Tolmie in 1826. Through her, her daughter Frances became familiar from earliest childhood with the music, poetry and history of the Western Highlands in the daily life of which her forebears have played so active a part; and, through a family and circle devoted to their country, she dwelt in constant touch with those traditions of which her song-collection gives us a delightful and unique glimpse.

The following books are amongst those which contain traditional matter and information of Miss Tolmie's collecting.

Leabhar na Feinne, heroic Gaelic ballads chiefly from 1512 to 1871, edited by J. F. Campbell of Islay (editor of *Tales of the West Highlands*), 1872; *Treatise on the Language, Poetry and Music of the Highland Clans*, by Donald Campbell, 1862; *The Gesto Collection of Highland Music*, 1895, and *Puirt-a-Beul*, 1901, both edited by Keith Norman Macdonald, M.D.; *Carmina Gadelica*, edited by Alexander Carmichael, LL.D.; *Songs of the Hebrides*, edited by Marjory Kennedy-Fraser and Kenneth Macleod; and the *Macdonald Collection of Gaelic Poetry*, edited by the Rev. Angus Macdonald, minister of Killearnan, and the Rev. Archibald Macdonald, minister of Kiltarlity, 1911; *Survivals in Belief among the Celts*, by George Henderson, M.A., B.Litt., Ph.D. (Vienna), Lecturer on Celtic Language and Literature in the University of Glasgow, 1911.

In this *Journal* Miss Tolmie has included several songs contributed by her to other publications. This has been done in order to present them here in their most complete and unaltered forms.

xii

In the case of some songs with many verses the Gaelic text already published has been omitted here, but references for it are given.

It is greatly to be regretted that space has not allowed us to reproduce Patrick M'Donald's essay on "The Influence of Poetry and Music upon the Highlanders" which follows the preface to *Highland Vocal Airs*, all noted by his brother before 1761, and published in 1781. *Highland Vocal Airs* is so rare a book that but few public libraries even in Scotland can boast a copy. The essay anticipates the best modern views concerning folk-song, and is of the greatest possible interest, inasmuch as it deals with the Ossianic poems, songs of occupation, the manner of singing them, and so forth, in a way that proves what strong links unite the Gaelic singers of to-day with those of a century and a half ago.

Patrick M'Donald would perhaps be surprised by the collection in this *Journal*, for he writes: "In less than twenty years, it would be vain to attempt a collection of Highland music. Perhaps it is rather late at present; but enough may be got to point out its genius and spirit." He adds "Different men will pursue different paths. The more of these, then, the better, provided the music is given genuine and unadulterated. It would be no difficult matter to make the airs more beautiful, and more agreeable to an improved ear, but, if this were done, there would be gross deceit in giving them as originals. Let them, therefore, appear in their native simplicity and nakedness; and, if improvements and variations shall be found necessary, these can be added afterwards. . . . To the philosophic antiquary, who contemplates with admiration every genuine fragment of the manners of ancient nations, those ancient airs will prove highly interesting. Peculiar manners, and peculiar music, though a subject of ridicule to the fastidious and illiberal, will be regarded by him as features, by which the Almighty hath distinguished nations (the great families of the earth) from each other."

Perhaps the Folk-Song Society may one day see its way to reprinting the very valuable essay from which the above is quoted.

Another matter for regret is that Miss Tolmie's collection did not appear in print a year or two earlier, so that Herr Bücher might have included specimens of genuine Gaelic songs of occupation in his *Arbeit und Rhythmus*. In this book he treats of working-songs from all quarters of the world, but, though striking parallels to our Gaelic songs of labour and the fashion of singing them are to be found in his book, the Highlands are not represented, and "Weel may the Keel row" seems to be the only example supplied to him by Great Britain! Herr Bücher's book throws the most interesting light possible upon these primitive songs, and certainly should be read in connection with this *Journal*.

The grateful thanks of the Folk-Song Society are offered to Miss Tolmie for allowing

xiii

part of her Gaelic traditional store to appear in its publications, and for the kind way in which she has faced the task of preparing the material for the press; also to the Rev. George Henderson, Ph.D., who has given invaluable help in reading Gaelic proofs and adding notes of interest to the songs. The Society is likewise greatly indebted to Miss A. G. Gilchrist for contributing her "Note on the Modal System of Gaelic Tunes," and for other help given in connection with the *Journal*.

The initials F. T. and G. H. attached to the annotations, stand for Miss Frances Tolmie and Dr. George Henderson; and L. E. B., A. G. G., and J. A. F. M. for Miss Lucy E. Broadwood, Miss A. G. Gilchrist and Mr. J. A. Fuller-Maitland, the editing Committee for this number.

LUCY E. BROADWOOD. [ED.]

NOTES AND REMINISCENCES.

BY FRANCES TOLMIE.

I WAS born in 1840, in the parish of Duirinish. Island of Skye, at Uignish Farm, of which my father, John Tolmie, was tacksman. After his death, in 1845, my mother and her family moved to the parish of Minginish, but later on we lived at the Manse of Bracadale and Ebost Farm. The places above referred to are all in "Macleod's Country" on the western side of Skye. My acquaintance with our native Gaelic poetry and music began with my life, and old songs are amongst my earliest recollections; but not till I had grown up did I realise that much with which I had been familiar throughout my youth was no longer regarded as in the order of the day. A great change had come over Bracadale within the preceding generation; the hereditary tacksmen, whose families had occupied the various farms for centuries, had emigrated, while many customs which had prevailed from time immemorial were no longer regularly observed and were fast becoming mere traditional memories for the young. For instance, the large gatherings, once held as a matter of course for the purpose of "waulking" or fulling homespun cloth, had ceased in most places, and "waulkings," together with the songs * that accompanied them, were seldom mentioned except by the older people in tones of regret, as belonging to an irrevocable past. I myself remembered them as of frequent occurrence in Minginish, and, for fear of losing these recollections and becoming a stranger even in my native country-side, I begged my mother to teach me some of the old songs which she learned in her youth. One of these, No. 62 in this collection, was a famous waulking-song in the Island of Eigg, where she was born. My brother, the minister of the parish, had a copy of Mackenzie's *Sàr Obair* or *Beauties of Gaelic Poetry*, and occasionally when the worthy schoolmaster, Mr. MacIntyre, came to spend the evening at the Manse, read aloud to him, or sang selections from the poetry of Alexander Macdonald and of Duncan Bàn MacIntyre, many of which I have never heard any one sing since, such as the "Praise of Ben Dóran" and Macdonald's waulking-song in praise of Mórag—the maiden under whose name he referred secretly to Prince Charlie—with many more. But at

---

* There seems to have been a vast common repertory of these waulking-songs throughout the Hebrides, from Kintyre to Sutherland.

that time I was not able to read Mackenzie's collection, as the subjects treated of were difficult for a girl of sixteen, and the language, not quite that of ordinary conversation, was made the more unattractive by frequent misprints. From a mistaken notion on the part of teachers, I had not been carefully taught to read and write Gaelic as part of my education, and I was but slowly advancing in my general knowledge by reading the Gaelic Bible. As time went on, I was asked to superintend some knitting which Miss Macleod of Macleod, often absent in London, had established among the women of the hamlets around. I accepted this office willingly, and thus, without seeking or planning, came into relation with those who could respond to my earnest wish to recall some of the forgotten songs of a by-gone age. My mother liking me to have an escort during my long rounds, our choice fell on Effie [or Oighrig] Ross, who lived alone in a bothy on the glebe, near a pretty waterfall known as "Am Forsan."* She was a kind creature, but wild-looking, and apt to turn crazy if unduly provoked; she had immense front teeth, tawny locks of hair strayed from beneath her cap over a high and peaked forehead, and her old skirts hung in fringed tatters over her bare feet. Effie's conversation usually turned on the ancient lore of the district, and to my extreme satisfaction she sang old waulking-songs as we went over the moor, carefully teaching me the refrains. She was elderly, but could not tell her age. When talking about the beauty of the world one day, she confessed to having gone down on her knees to a magnificent cloud overhead, stating her conviction that in doing so she had not committed a sin. She has long been dead, together with the other dear women whose names are recorded on my list of singers. Had there been an old head on my youthful shoulders, much more would have been drawn from the fountain of Effie's memory—but my vision was then limited, and I learned only what she selected to teach me. When my mother moved to Ebost, three miles from the Manse, I had as my walking companion little Margaret Gillies [Mairearad bheag, nighean Domhnuill 'ic Ruairidh = Little Margaret, daughter of Donaldson-of-Rory], also an elderly person, living alone in a bothy on the verge of the moor. Though a tame character in comparison with Effie, she had the same pleasure in singing and teaching any song that took my fancy. In those days—1860-2—in Bracadale, or over in Minginish when on a visit to my early home under the Coolin range, I occasionally met Dr. Alex. Carmichael (editor and translator of *Carmina Gadelica*), who encouraged my interest in the old songs, and advised me to note down the tunes to them. When anything uncommon came under my observation I sent a copy of it to Miss Macleod of Macleod, who understood Gaelic and sympathised with the new movement, earnestly aided by Professor Blackie of Edinburgh, for the

---

* Name of Norse origin, meaning "the waterfall"; the Gaelic article *am* was prefixed at a later period when the Norse significance had been forgotten.—G. H.

preservation of the culture of the Gael. All the songs I learned from my associates were of one special class : those helpful in forms of work requiring the united effort of groups of persons, such as rowing, reaping, and the waulking of cloth ; wild chants not without a certain feeling for true composition in the simple words and airs, with a reminiscence in them of a grandeur for ever gone, and a suggestion of deep regret which touched the heart without artificial aid. These songs made their truest effect when heard in the tremulous tones of age, beside the smouldering peat-fire under some lowly roof.

In the year 1868 my mother moved her household to Nairn, on the eastern side of Scotland, whence we sometimes revisited Skye, staying at Portree, where in 1870 I became acquainted with "Mairearad Mhór" (or "Tall Margaret") Macleod, who lived alone in a bothy near the Great Moss, and maintained herself by knitting and spinning. When she came to the house of my sister, about some work, she occasionally remained to spend the evening with the maids, who delighted in her witty and amusing stories. I would be invited to join the party in the kitchen to hear Margaret sing, and learned from her several pieces with appropriate tunes, such as I have never heard from any other person but herself, with the exception of Mrs. M'Vicar (Harriet or "Herrot") in North Uist. She sang in a solemn and tragic manner as if she had herself witnessed the scenes described in the versified narratives (cf. Nos. 88, 85, 86, 87), fragments of longer compositions transmitted orally from a remote past, and acquired by her in youth, when hearing her father and other old men chanting them by the fireside on winter nights. "Ha !" exclaims Mary Ross, "every man sits down to read a newspaper nowadays when evening sets in, and the heroic songs are no longer remembered."

In 1872, at Contin Manse, happening to open a somewhat tattered volume on my brother's shelf I discovered that this was a collection of Gaelic songs, compiled by Gillies in 1786, and found among the contents the lays above cited, of which I had learned some verses and the tunes from "Tall Margaret." A scholar will understand why I read very little from that book : it was in a somewhat difficult diction, with dialect words, and not free from mistakes in spelling.

In the year 1871 I visited my cousins, John Macdonald and Mrs. M'Neill, at Newton Farm, North Uist, and there met another interesting person, Mrs. Duncan M'Vicar, known by her friends as "Herrott" (for "Harriet," she having been so named after a lady of Lord Macdonald's family). She was a widow who supported herself by spinning. Mrs. M'Neill invited me to the kitchen to see Herrot, and I found a great deal going on there : the spinning-wife was at one side of the apartment, sitting at her wheel ready for conversation ; a weaver had arrived, and, having set up a frame, was warping a new web on the opposite side ; the cook was busy over the fire, and so was the dairymaid with affairs of her own department ; and, to be free from interruption, Herrot and I were sent up to a garret to talk and sing. And there I learned from her part of the "Song of Praise to

Donald Gorm" (No. 78), the "Lament for Diarmid," and other waulking-songs bearing on the nobility, the courage, and generosity of Clan Donald. "Herrott" M'Vicar, who was tall, grey, and elderly like Margaret M'Leod, sang in the same manner, with great reverence as about a sacred subject. On returning to Skye I must have given copies of these words to Miss Macleod of Macleod, who was then staying at Gesto in Bracadale. Afterwards, when I was at Nairn, Miss Macleod wrote to say that Campbell of Islay meant to call on me about a tune to one of the songs which I had learned in Uist; but affairs hurried him to the south, and I never heard again of the matter. In 1873 I went to England, and remained there for many years. But in 1895 when living at Oban, I happened, whilst visiting Edinburgh, to be at 25 Geo. IV. Bridge, the shop of Mr. Norman Macleod, publisher and bookseller, and there found an old copy of *Leabhar nu Fèinne (the Book of the Fèinn*)*, by J. F. Campbell of Islay, 1872, which was out of print. Having secured it I examined its contents at leisure, and found some of the lines which I had given to Miss Macleod so many years before: versions of the "Lament for Diarmid," and the "Warning of Ossian to his Mother," much popularised to suit the simple requirements of the company seated at the waulking-board.

In the year 1900, when spending a day at Dr. Alex. Carmichael's house at Taynuilt, near Loch Awe, I met Dr. George Henderson. In the course of conversation, and after I had been singing some "Puirt-a-Beul,"† both friends expressed a wish that I would write down all the tunes I remembered; this I promised to do, on condition that they would get the gaps in my verses filled up. Ultimately, Dr. Henderson introduced me to Miss Lucy Broadwood of the Folk-Song Society, to whom I am greatly indebted for the opportunity of uniting scattered memories into a whole which may serve some purpose for illustration and comparison, even though the songs may never more be sung in this world. No songs here given have been taken from books. ‡ All—texts and tunes —were learned by me from the singers who have preserved them by tradition. I know several of Mary Macleod's songs, but the airs to Nos. 98 and 99 seem to have been hitherto unrecorded and I never heard any one but "little Margaret" sing them. A version of their words I later found in Mackenzie's *Sàr Obair*, but I hear them sung nowhere to-day. No. 43, taught me by "little Margaret" and Roderick M'Leod, had never been taken down before. The songs of Effie Ross were already nearly forgotten by the people in 1860, and amongst my contemporaries my pleasure in these old wives' songs was considered very odd, for they were not deemed "poetry" or worthy of notice by song-collectors of that period.   FRANCES TOLMIE.

* The Fingalians or the followers of Fionn mac Cumhail : the heroes of the Ossianic Cycle of Celtic Saga.

† Literally "mouth-tunes," sung as a substitute for instrumental dance-music by the Highlanders. "Domhnull Cìbeir" ("Donald the Shepherd"), who married our nurse, Kate M'Swein, used to sing "puirt-a-beul" to us little ones.—F. T.

‡ Except a few lines of "'Phiuthrag nam Piuthar" (No. 21), quoted from *Transactions of the Gaelic Society of Inverness*.

A SINGER'S MEMORIES OF LIFE IN SKYE.

MARY ROSS, known in her native hamlet as Màiri Rànuill, was born, probably about the year 1848, at Killmaluag in Skye, not far from Duntulm Castle, which, though now in ruins, was for several generations a residence of the Chiefs of Clan Donald. Her much-respected father, Ranald Ross, named in the native speech "Rànull Buidhe" ("Ranald of the yellow hair"), had a croft there which he worked with industry and intelligent method. His wife having died when his children were very young (Mary the eldest being only seven years of age), he married a young woman who was a weaveress and devoted much time to her loom, the care of the younger children devolving on Mary. It was in the loving fulfilment of her duty at home that Mary remained familiar with cradle-songs and "puirt-a-beul" (vocal tunes for dancing or quick movement). When out on the pasture with her young charges, she used to meet an old man herding cows. He told her many a tale of long ago, and sang quaint rhymes which are now almost forgotten. Many of her songs she acquired when running about the hamlet with her playmates, and entering the neighbours' houses. If her gentle grandfather, an old soldier of the Peninsular War, happened to be within, the general conversation often turned on by-gone times, and events were commemorated by songs. Or at the inn, when her father, grandfather, and other estimable men might be sitting round a table in friendly conversation, singing in innocence of heart as the bottle went round, she heard and learned from them the sea-songs of Alexander Macdonald, the lays expressive of his loyalty to Prince and Chief [Clanranald] in 1745, and the equally appealing strains of Duncan Bàn MacIntyre, telling of the tender loveliness and grandeur of mountain and moor ere the noble deer had been in many places supplanted by sheep. At home, in the long winter evenings, by the light of a brilliant peat-fire in the middle of the floor or of a "crusie" fed with a wick and home-made fish-oil, her father spent his hours of leisure in repairing the harness of his horse, in plaiting matting of grass or straw for various purposes, in mending nets or twisting heather-ropes. Then he would croon to himself solemn chants from the ancient lays of Ossianic times—lays which were regarded with reverence by the young folk because this grave, usually silent parent sang them, but which were too serious for them to learn and remember well in years to come. In connection with her step-mother's occupation Mary was wont to hear music of another character, when a waulking * (or fulling) of cloth was

* *Cf.* Danish "valke" and German "walken" = to full (cloth).

147

held at her home or at a neighbour's house, long before she was invited to take her place at the board. Her step-mother wove homespun in various forms, such as "kelt,"* grey, blue, or ruddy-brown, drugget for women's skirts, flannel, blankets, and bed-covers; the wool having been dyed, carded, spun into yarn and wound, before it was sent to her. Mary remembers the first time she assisted at a waulking, when another girl and she were placed beside a remarkable old woman who was to take the leading part in the singing but was not expected to touch the cloth. They sat one on each side to support her, at about the middle of the board, while she poured forth one song after another; occasionally, according to custom, adding witty, satirical or amusing lines applicable to members of the audience.† Young men were there, as usual, and even grave elderly men did not think it beneath their dignity to be present when this woman, possessed of a wonderful memory and knowledge of fine passages of ancient poetry, was to sing. It was believed that her mother, a native of Lewis, and full of lore, had imparted it all to her, together with her skill in certain magical practices for which the people of Lewis were renowned.

A waulking, while a useful and necessary domestic function, was also regarded as a pleasant form of entertainment. Invitations were issued, and the obliging guests came dressed neatly and specially for the occasion, with bare arms and stout aprons. They took their places—six to ten persons on each side, leaving elbow-room—at the waulking-table. This was a long board about three feet in width, grooved lengthways, and resting on trestles. The cloth to be fulled or thickened was slowly dealt out from a vat at one end of the board. This vat, which contained a special liquid, was presided over by the good-wife of the house or some other person of experience. The wet mass of cloth was firmly grasped by one of the waulkers and pushed towards the person opposite, who with a similar gesture returned it to be sent on to the next opposing pair. This process continued till the cloth had gone the round of the board three or four times. When the moisture in it had been duly absorbed, the cloth was plunged again into the vat "to get a

---

* In early Irish *celt* means "raiment, covering." The word "tweed" for homespun or "kelt" was unknown in those days.—F. T.

In the Old Irish text, *Togail Bruidne Dá Derga*, it occurs in this sense; from it Stokes rightly derived English "kilt," as well as the Irish formation *dechalt*, "a cloak and shirt" (Cormac's *Glossary*); Kuno Meyer (*Contributions to Irish Lexicography*) gives the primary meaning as "hair."—G. H.

† The improvising of verses in which fun is freely made of those present, or known to the company, is probably the survival of some very primitive custom in connection with preparing material for clothing. Bücher, in his *Arbeit und Rhythmus* (Leipzig, 1909), at pp. 74-83, gives an account of the pulling up and preparing of flax by German peasants, to songs in which those present are satirised and the names of local young men and maidens connected in joke; rhythmical chorus and solo alternating. In Switzerland similar chaffing songs are the custom at hemp-dressing parties amongst the Grison peasants (*Schweizerisches Archiv für Volkskunde*, 14ter Jahrgang, i.). Mungo Park has described the improvised song of negresses during cotton-spinning, himself being the subject of it.—L. E. B.

drink" and go the round of the board again until pronounced thick enough. Singing accompanied the process throughout, songs of slow and solemn character (such as Nos. 88 and 89) coming first, followed by those in quicker time and merrier (*see* Nos. 60 and 62). Towards the close a slow measure (such as Nos. 75 and 45) was again used. The new web received its final treatment to the accompaniment of a solemn strain of song (*see* Nos. 98 and 43). During the singing of it the cloth was slowly and carefully wound round a board used to press it and give it a finish. According to Dr. A. Carmichael, this final process concludes still in some places with devout magical movements and words of benediction on the future wearer.*

The waulking-song differed from the "duanag" or ditty, in that its solo verse-part, consisting usually of but one line, though sometimes of two, was often (but not invariably) followed by a little refrain in meaningless syllables, and was succeeded by the chorus, in which all present—both workers and audience—joined. I once met a woman in North Uist who told me that the doctor had advised her to frequent waulkings as the best remedy against mental depression, from which she suffered.

There seems to have been no fixed rule as to the point at which the waulking-songs began, whether with the solo or the chorus (*cf.* Nos. 88, 89, 44, 45, 60, 62, etc.). A continuous round was kept up of the three parts (solo verse, solo refrain, and chorus) with no very marked ending. The reaping- and rowing-songs proceeded in the same manner, were often heard at waulkings, and were usually included in the singer's traditional repertory. As to other music, there was no dancing at Killmaluag in Mary's youth, but the ordinary expression of gladness and sympathy when a wedding occurred could not be suppressed, and neighbours met at the house of the bride's family and sang joyous songs. The company when singing sat in a circle, each member of which was linked to the next by means of a handkerchief held at the ends between them.† The rhythm of the songs was vigorously marked by the waving up and down of the handkerchiefs in unison.

FRANCES TOLMIE.

* For example: On seeing a young man receive a new suit it was proper to salute him thus: "Gum meal thu e; gun caith thu e, 's gum faigh thu bean r'a linn!" ("May'st thou enjoy it: may'st thou wear it, and find a wife the while!")—G. H.

† This mode of singing is common still in the Arisaig district of Inverness-shire.—L. E. B.

NOTE ON THE MODAL SYSTEM OF GAELIC TUNES.

BY ANNIE G. GILCHRIST.

AT the suggestion of Mr. J. A. Fuller-Maitland, who concurs in my opinion regarding the pentatonic foundation of the tunes in this collection, I have collected various annotations of certain tunes into the form of a preface, with some diffidence, and disclaiming any wish to dogmatise. This prefatory note forms, indeed, no more than a suggestion which may or may not be accepted by musicians possessing a wider acquaintance with the obscure and debatable subject of scales.

A distinct line of demarcation may be observed between the music of the Highlands and Lowlands of Scotland, coinciding with the frontier lines of language and nationality. The folk-songs of the two races differ rhythmically, as the construction and poetical system of the two languages differ—emotionally, as the characters of the Gael and Lowlander differ—and finally differ in scale; for Gaelic vocal music clings more or less to its ancient gapped scale, and retains a characteristic avoidance of certain notes, whereas Lowland-Scottish music now approximates in its seven-note modal construction to the folk-music of England. Lowland music has, however, been greatly enriched by borrowings from Gaelic sources.

Almost all the tunes in the present most valuable and interesting collection are in a gapped scale; there are but some dozen or so, amongst the whole number, which contain seven degrees, the remainder being in a two-gapped or one-gapped scale—the latter a modification of the former, and slightly predominating in number. And there is not, I consider, a single tune in the whole collection really corresponding with either our modern major or minor scale.

It has hitherto been generally assumed that the two-gapped, *i.e.* five-note, Scottish scale, known as the "Scottish pentatonic scale," is equivalent to our scale of C major, with the 4th and 7th degrees absent; but a careful examination of the tunes in this happily genuine and undoctored collection has led me to the conclusion that this primitive pentatonic scale was rather equivalent to the scale of C to C with the *3rd* and 7th degrees omitted (possibly built upon the three fifths, C-G, D-A, F-C):

FIG. 1.   No 3rd.   No 7th.

This is the scale upon which many Highland "iorrams" (of which the "Skye Boat Song" is a good and well-known example) and other songs of labour are constructed, with or without the upper C to form the complete pentatonic scale (E and B♭ occur occasionally as non-essential notes in some of these tunes). Probably in such songs of labour we get very near the beginnings of a nation's folk-music. *Cf.* "Oran do Dhomnull Gorm," No. 78 in this collection, also the primitive melody of the waulking-song "Oran Arabhaig," No. 74, founded on the four notes known as the "Westminster" or "Cambridge" chimes. The sea-chanty, "Tom's gone to Ilo" (*see* Tozer's *Sailor Songs,* and also variants in the *Journal*) is another example of a tune made on the above pentatonic scale, which corresponds to the later Chinese pentatonic scale (*see* Sir Hubert Parry's *History of Music,* chapter on "Scales"), and these five notes appear to me to form the nucleus of Highland music. (The characteristic quality of Gaelic song might even be reduced to this succession of notes:

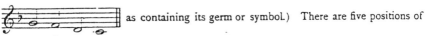 as containing its germ or symbol.) There are five positions of

which the pentatonic scale above noted (Fig. 1) is susceptible. Taking C, D, F, G and A respectively as "tonics," five pentatonic modes are formed, practically equivalent to the late Dr. Culwick's five Irish pentatonic modes of the "1st Period" (*see* his lecture on *Ancient Irish Melody,* 1897), and to the five Scottish pentatonic modes noted in Helmholtz's *Sensations of Tone* (translated by Dr. A. J. Ellis), though not arranged in the same order as either series. So far, though noted in different order and pitch, these three schemes of modes really correspond, *so long as no question be raised as to whether the missing intervals be ♭, ♯ or ♮.* It is in the later bridging of the gaps by filling in the missing notes that the Scottish and Irish modes appear to me to become differentiated. Dr. Culwick fills in the 4th and 7th of his scale:

FIG. 2.

with F♯ and B♮. According to my schedule of Scottish modes (*q.v.* below) the gaps, D to F and A to C, become in time filled by a doubtful E, natural or flattened (which, for convenience, will be called E♯), and by B♭. In the working out of these two now diverging theories, Dr. Culwick arrives at five seven-note modes on C, D, E, G and A, corresponding to Lydian (which he calls "the fully formed Irish scale"), Mixolydian, Aeolian, Ionian and Dorian ; whereas, according to my theory of the development of Scottish-Gaelic pentatonic modes, similar bridging eventually produces modes in scale resembling Mixolydian, Aeolian, Ionian, a rare and doubtful Dorian (owing to the uncertainty of its 6th degree), and a Phrygian mode—the last being a mode not located in Irish music by Dr. Culwick, but one of which there are several more or less fully developed examples in the present collection. On the other hand, I have been unable to find a single instance of his Lydian mode in Scottish music, Which, so far, confirms this theory of divergence. That tunes in more or less fully developed modes of six and seven notes are to be found amongst Gaelic music is, as I consider, due, as shown above, to the gradual filling up of the gapped scale in its five positions, either by a natural development, which one may believe to trace in those tunes in which the gaps are bridged by unessential notes—probably indeterminate in the first instance, and of the nature of grace-notes—or by contact with a seven-note system in English and Lowland-Scottish folk-music. The preference for the B♭ instead of the B♮, when the note does begin to creep into the pentatonic scale above noted, is, I think, sufficient to account for the almost total absence of examples suggesting the Dorian amongst these further-developed modes, though a likeness to the Ecclesiastical Mixolydian, Aeolian and Phrygian modes becomes apparent in tunes where the B♭ appears as the minor 7th, minor 6th, and minor 2nd respectively of the mode, as well as a resemblance to the modern major mode when it appears as the 4th degree. A mode resembling the Dorian would, of course, be produced by the similar filling-in with B♭ and E♮ of the gaps in the pentatonic mode beginning on G—the fourth position of the above-written scale (Fig. 1), (as also by the flattening of the E in the first mode beginning on C), but I have not observed any fully developed Gaelic examples of this mode, the 3rd and 6th being seldom both present in the same tune. (If space permitted, illustrations might be given of pentatonic, and presumably earlier, forms of Scottish airs which have acquired a stereotyped heptatonic form in printed collections.)

The Scottish preference for B♭ instead of B♮ may possibly be connected with an obscure passage in the continuation of Fordun's *Scotichronicon* (quoted in the original mediæval Latin in Hawkins' *History of Music*, Book XIII., p. 562) alluding to the use of "Bemol" amongst Scottish harpers : "*seu Diatesserone seu Diapente cordæ concrepent, semper tenera Bemol incipiunt et in Bemol redeunt*"—a passage which has a curious parallel in a description by Giraldus Cambrensis (recently quoted by Mr. A. P. Graves) of the musical performances of his Welsh compatriots, in which, after speaking of the singers as employing "many modes and measures," he describes them as "agreeing at last with organic melody in one harmony under the sweet influence of B♭." However one may interpret these passages, they certainly seem to point to the fact of the note B♭ being employed in Scottish and Welsh music of a period contemporaneous with each writer quoted, though uncultured singers must have adhered more or less to their pentatonic scale for some time after the introduction of this note, as is shown by surviving instances of such adherence.

As regards this conservation of the older scale, Sir Hubert Parry may be quoted on pentatonic scales in general. "Nearly all the pentatonic scales," he says, "have been

THE FIVE MODES OF THE SCOTTISH PENTATONIC SCALE.

	MODE 1.	MODE 2.	MODE 3.	MODE 4.	MODE 5.
PENTATONIC.	No 3rd. No 7th.	No 2nd. No 6th.	No 4th. No 7th.	No 3rd. No 6th.	No 2nd. No 5th.
6-NOTE SCALE. *a*	No 3rd. No 7th.	* No 6th. [Very common.]	No 4th. *	No 3rd.	No 2nd.
6-NOTE SCALE. *b*	No 3rd.	No 2nd.	No 7th.	No 6th.	No 5th.
	a + *b* = Aeolian.	*a* + *b* = Ionian. (With E♭ = Mixolydian.)		*a* + *b* = Dorian.	*a* + *b* = Phrygian.

* *The E is sometimes flattened in these three modes, more especially when occurring as the 7th degree of Mode 3.   See note on No. 29.*

Note.—The distinction between "Mode 1, *a*" and "Mode 3, *b*," which appear to correspond in scale, lies in whether the 3rd or the 4th degree of the mode be an essential note, belonging to the original pentatonic framework.   Similarly, in the case of "Mode 2, *a*" and "Mode 4, *b*," the distinction lies in whether the 2nd or 3rd degree be the imported note.   This is the principle upon which tunes have been assigned to one or other mode.   The five *essential* scale-notes and the one secondary bridge-note can usually be identified with ease in a tune in a one-gapped (*i.e.* six-note) mode, and, when found, locate that mode.

The characteristic Highland mode formed by the filling-up of the gaps in Mode 1 by E♮ and F♮ is distinct in tonality from the Mixolydian Mode, whose scale it resembles; it corresponds more nearly to the Hypo-Ionian, owing to the prominence of F and A, its 4th and 6th degrees.   The plagal effect of the oscillation between C and F is very noticeable in tunes in this peculiarly Scottish mode.   *Cf.* the "Oran do Mhac-Griogair a Ruadh-shruth," No. 97 in this collection, in which there are two endings, one in this mode, on C (probably the older), and one on F, in Mode 3.—A. G. G.

filled in, and the nations who use them are familiar with other notes besides the curious and characteristic formula of five; but in the background of their musical feeling the original foundation of their system remains distinct."

A schedule of the Gaelic Pentatonic Modes, arranged according to my suggested notation of them, each with its two derivative six-note modes, is appended. I have classified the tunes of Miss Tolmie's collection in accordance with this, referring each to one or other of the modes in this table. No doubt there will be differences of opinion regarding classification in the case of some tunes, especially those in which the modes are mixed, and certain others in which it is difficult to believe that the last note of the tune is the true tonic (*see* note to "Till an Crodh," No. 28). In examining the tunes in MS., there was also some uncertainty in certain cases as to where the tune really ended, owing to the fact of the song beginning with the chorus or refrain.* The order of the "*a*" and "*b*" six-note modes is not meant to be chronological, though the probability is that the B7 was the later note to come into the scale, from the fact that it is still the one most frequently missing, *e.g.* "Pentatonic Mode 2 (*a*)" is very common. Nor is it intended to represent the six-note modes as fixed or fully developed in character. But written out as below they form a convenient index to the modifications of the pentatonic scale on its way towards a seven-note system. In conclusion, it may be said that the "highly artificial" scale of the Scottish bagpipe appears to have exercised little influence on Gaelic folk-song. A pentatonic basis has been claimed for the bagpipe scale, but this seems very doubtful. It appears more probable that this curious scale belongs to an ancient seven-note system of eastern origin. The instrument itself, known to Chaucer's England, seems to have come into general favour in Scotland about the close of the fifteenth century.

A. G. GILCHRIST.

BAZIL POINT, SOUTHPORT.
    June. 1911.

* Some of these tunes, being of the 'circular' class, have *no* definite ending.

ADDITIONAL NOTE ON THE GAELIC SCALE SYSTEM.

BY LUCY E. BROADWOOD.

IN connection with Miss Gilchrist's interesting theories, which appear to me to offer a sound and clear solution of much that is usually obscure to the student of primitive scales and melody, may be read the section headed rather significantly "Persia, Arabia, Syria, and Scottish Highlands" in the late Dr. A. J. Ellis's *Musical Scales of Various Nations* (*Journal of the Society of Arts*, March 27th, 1885). I venture to suggest that it throws some light on the existence of the B flat in Celtic music.

Dr. Ellis gives us the Persian and Arabic scale-systems as set forth in the writings of Al Farabi (*d.* A.D. 950). From this it appears that the Persian lute had four, and subsequently five, strings. Each successive string was tuned a fourth higher than the next lower; the fingerboard being fretted with three ligatures, so as to give the Greek tetrachord on each string. The series of fourths would produce C, F, B♭, E♭, A♭ on the open strings. These notes, when arranged to form a scale, give precisely Mode 5 of Miss Gilchrist's schedule. The subjoined tune, which is probably the original Highland source of the very old air used by Burns for his song, "A Highland Lad my Love was born," exemplifies this mode.

CUIR A NALL DUINN AM BOTAL.

Noted by L. E. Broadwood.
Mode 5. (No 2nd or 5th.)

SUNG BY CATRIONA M'LEAN,
ARISAIG DISTRICT, INVERNESS-SHIRE, 1907.

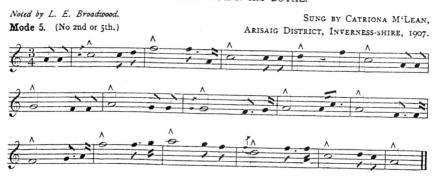

I have a very melodious bamboo pipe, made by a Sicilian peasant after the pattern in common use by the country-folk of Sicily. This is pierced with six holes for the fingers and two for the thumbs. The result is a gapped scale: F, A♭, B♭, D♭, E♭, F 8ᵛᵉ (and with the top thumb-hole open also an A♭ 8ᵛᵉ). This scale gives precisely the same intervals as Miss Gilchrist's Gaelic Mode 5, pentatonic form, and the Persian or Arabic scale, and it probably derives from the Arab settlers in Sicily. Gaelic tunes can be played with especial ease upon this reed pipe, I find. The late accurate authority, Mr. A. J. Hipkins, was for many years Dr. Ellis's constant collaborator in scientific musical research. Himself a Highlander by descent, and in close touch with Gaelic subjects, Mr. Hipkins was fond of pointing out the striking likeness between the Arabic and Highland scales (see *Musical Scales of Various Nations* also on the Oriental scale and origin of the European bagpipes). If those ethnologists are right who maintain that the West Highlands were originally peopled by a Mediterranean-Iberian stock, similarity between the Gaelic, Sicilian and Oriental scales need hardly surprise us.

L. E. BROADWOOD.

LONDON, 1911.

THE SINGERS.

ANDERSON, Janet (Seònaid), native of the parish of Strath, Skye. Nurse for many years at the Manses of Bracadale, Skye, and Contin, Ross-shire. Elderly in 1871.

BEATON, Effie (Oighrig), cottar, at Ebost, Bracadale, Skye. Of advanced age in 1860.

CAMERON, Miss Isabel, from Laggan-Ulva, Isle of Mull, who learned old songs and rhymes from her aged nurse, a native of Eigg.

GILLIES, Margaret ("Mairearad bheag, nigh'n Domhnuill 'ic Ruairidh" or "Little Margaret, daughter of Donald, son of Rory"), cottar at Ebost, Bracadale, Skye. Elderly in 1862.

MACDIARMID, Kate, cottar, spinner and knitter, Minginish, Skye. Elderly, and acting as nurse, in 1866.

MACDONALD, Mrs. Archibald, crofter in Eigg. Elderly in 1902.

M'DOUGALL, Jessie, from Moidart, Inverness-shire. Living at Nairn, and 25 years old, in 1870.

M'KENZIE, Mrs. Hector, from Dunvegan, Duirinish, Skye, 1865.

MACLACHLAN, Mr., crofter at Dervaig, Isle of Mull, 1902.

M'LEAN, Mrs., wife of crofter and fisherman, Barra.

M'LEOD, Margaret ("Mairearad Mhór" or "Tall Margaret"), cottar, spinner and knitter, Portree, Skye. Elderly in 1871.

MACLEOD, Mr. Neil, from Glendale, Duirinish, Skye. Son of Donald Macleod, the famous Skye bard ; and himself foremost amongst Gaelic bards of the present day. Author of *Clàrsach an Doire* (1883), etc. In May, 1911, was presented with a testimonial from his countrymen scattered all over the world. Has retired recently after forty years of work as agent for the firm of Messrs. R. & R. Macleod, tea merchants, Edinburgh and London.

MACLEOD, Roderick, cottar at Ebost, Bracadale, Skye. Very old, and bent low when singing the low note in song No. 43.

MacNEILL, Mrs., Newton Farm, North Uist.

MacNEILL, Margaret (" Peigidh Bhanachaig " or " Peggy Dairymaid"). On wild nights, with whirring wheel, a loving singer of incomprehensible, "old, unhappy far-off things"—sung in deep, croaking tones—by the bedside of a favourite little friend in Minginish, Skye, in 1845. In the year 1862 she contributed some lines to song No. 50. Died at Borreraig, Skye, in 1896 ; aged nearly 100.

MACPHERSON, Mary, poetess, from Trotternish, Skye. Elderly in 1871.

MacVICAR, Mrs. Duncan (" Herrot "= Harriet), spinner and knitter, North Uist. Not unlike Margaret Macleod, and, like her, versed in old lore generally. Elderly in 1871.

ROSS, Effie (Oighrig), cottar, native of Waternish, but spent the greater part of her life in Bracadale, Skye. Rather feeble-minded in practical life, but with a poetical soul.

ROSS, Mary (Màiri Rànuill), from Killmaluag, in Trotternish, Skye. Elderly in 1909, and living then in Edinburgh.

TOLMIE, Mrs. John (Margaret MacAskill), born at Kildonan, Eigg, in 1808 ; died at Oban, 1889. Lived her married life at Uignish on Loch Dunvegan, Skye. Mother of the collector of these songs, and the singer of those marked as early or nursery recollections in Minginish, Bracadale and at Ebost.

[NOTE : CH., S., R., and V. throughout the following songs stands for Chorus, Solo, Refrain and Verse respectively. S. R. stands for "solo refrain." The manner in which these usually alternate is referred to on p. 149 of this Journal. The verse-lines are sung *solo*, and whether the song opens with the verse, solo refrain, or chorus, the second verse begins at the same point of the music as verse 1, and so on throughout, on the pattern of the complete verse given to the music.]

GROUP I.—SONGS OF REST AND RECREATION.

CRADLE SONGS.

1.—UAMH 'N ÒIR (i.).

(THE CAVE OF GOLD.)

An Early Nursery Memory,
Skye.—F. T.

Mode 1. *a. è.*

1. Mu 'n till mis - e, mu 'n ruig mis - e; Mu 'n till mis - e a Uamh 'n Oir.

TRANSLATION.

1. Ere I return, ere I attain, ere I return from Uamh 'n Òir 2. the young of the goats will be goats of the crags, and the little calves become great kine. 3. Creel-bearing horses will be riding-steeds, and babes, borne in the bosom, men, bearing arms. But never more shall I return.

The tradition relating to Uamh 'n Òir has for many generations been the subject of various lullabies throughout the Hebrides. The entrance to the cave is at Harlosh, near the shore, a few miles to the south-west of Dunvegan in Skye.

Long ago, an exploring party accompanied by a piper entered this cavern, expecting to find a subterranean passage which should lead them in an easterly direction quite across the island to another cave bearing the same name of Uamh 'n Òir, near Monkstadt in Trotternish. Some hours after the men set out on this adventure, a woman sitting at the well of Tulaich (Tobar Tulaich), near Harlosh, heard coming up through the water the voice of the piper, in despairing tones expressing a wish that he might have three hands—two for the bagpipe, and one for the sword with which to fight the monster that presumably overcame his companions and himself, who were never seen nor heard of again. Tobar Tulaich was a sacred well, believed to possess magical health-restoring properties and to be the best water in Skye. The people of Trotternish had a similar belief about the well of Lianacro, not far from the other cave in Trotternish. The songs have kept the legend in remembrance to our day; four of them were contributed by me to the *Gesto Coll.* (App. p. 23), and *Puirt-a-beul*, pp. 47 and 48. The tunes are here given for the first time in their complete forms, but the full Gaelic text, being in the publications just cited, is not given here.—F. T.

I have heard a similar legend of the same cave and a piper who never returned, which according to my recollection was connected with the well-known air called "Macrimmon's Lament." The piper, either alone, or preceding the rest of the party, entered the cave playing this lament, with its mournful refrain, "Cha till, cha till, cha till mi tuille"—(Return! return! return—ah, never!) the sound of his pipes growing fainter as he penetrated further into the cave. Presently a despairing cry was heard: "If it were not for the great grey (she) one—!" And the rest was silence.

The inference naturally drawn from these legends is that the music of the piper acted as a charm or protection, and that ceasing playing, in order to defend himself, he perished.—A. G. G.

The Highland Bagpipe, its History, Literature and Music, by Manson (A. Gardner, Paisley, 1901), now unfortunately out of print, has an interesting chapter on "Pipers in enchanted caves." The incident in the above song is located in several places—Skye, Mull and Inverness-shire more especially. In connection with the protective power of music read the fifth chapter of Jules Combarieu's *La Musique, ses lois et son évolution.*—L. E. B.

Gold (*or*, genitive *òir*, from Latin *aurum*) is symbolical of hidden treasure, which legend often and naturally associates with caves. The scene of the incidents in the "Lay of the Great Fool" is laid at Dùn-an-Òir, where, according to one version, Fionn was slain, where Connal avenged the death of Cuchulainn, where Caoilte fought his best fight (Campbell's *Leabhar na Féinne*, p. 203). For a Gaelic legend associating this cave with the Macrimmon pipers see *The Celtic Monthly* for 1910, p. 46. About twenty years ago I met a very old woman in Uist who told me this legend as "a fact in the life of one of her ancestors."—G. H.

2.—UAMH 'N ÒIR (ii.).

(THE CAVE OF GOLD.)

PENTATONIC.   LEARNT IN EARLY CHILDHOOD (1846),
Mode 2.   SKYE.—F. T.
 Slow.   *Fine.*

Chaill mo làmh a lùths! Chaill mo làmh a lùths! Chaill mo làmh a lùths! Thréig an Lùd-ag mi!

TRANSLATION.

My hand has lost its power [*repeat twice*]. And my little finger is gone.

158

In *Puirt-a-beul*, to which I contributed words and air, the tune has been omitted. The words are on p. 47. For explanation of the song *see* the notes at the end of "Uamh 'n Òir" (i.) in this Journal.—F. T.

3.—UAMH 'N ÒIR (iii.).

(THE CAVE OF GOLD.)

PENTATONIC.
Mode 1.

A NURSERY RECOLLECTION,
SKYE, 1845.—F. T.

1. Mo dhìth, mo dhìth gun trì làmh-an. Mo dhìth, mo dhìth gun trì làmh-an, Dà làimh 'sa phìob, dà làimh 'sa phìob, Dà làimh 'sa phìob, 's làmh 'sa chlaidh-eamh.

TRANSLATION.

1. My loss, my loss that I lack three hands! [*twice*]. Two hands to the bag-pipe [*thrice*] and one to the sword. 2. Grievous my state without three hands! [*twice*]. Two hands, etc., etc.

See notes on "Uamh 'n Òir" (i.)—F. T.

4.—UAMH 'N OIR (iv.).

(THE CAVE OF GOLD.)

LEARNT IN CHILDHOOD,
SKYE.—F. T.

Mode 3. *b.* (6-note scale.)

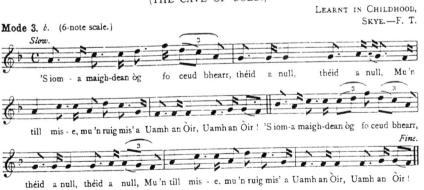

'S iom - a maigh-dean òg fo ceud bhearr, théid a null, théid a null, Mu 'n till mis - e, mu 'n ruig mis' a Uamh an Òir, Uamh an Òir! 'S iom-a maigh-dean òg fo ceud bhearr, théid a null, théid a null, Mu 'n till mis - e, mu 'n ruig mis' a Uamh an Òir, Uamh an Òir!

B

Many a youthful maiden, bearing her first growth of hair, will go over, will go over, ere I return, ere I arrive from Uamh 'n Òir.

The above air, with Gaelic words, contributed by me, is in the *Gesto Coll.* (App. p. 23). For notes on the legend *see* "Uamh 'n Òir" (i.) in this Journal.—F. T.

This, termed in the *Gesto Coll.* a "pibroch," seems allied strongly to the Irish tune, "The Eagle's Whistle" (*see Petrie Coll.,* Joyce's *Ancient Irish Music,* and *Journal F.S.S.* vol. ii. No. 10). The printed Irish airs, though said to be for marching, are all in three-four time, but Dr. Joyce has lately noted a version in four time, which would bring this Gaelic air more into line with the Irish tune.—L. E. B.

5.—ORAN TÀLAIDH AN EICH-UISGE.

(THE LULLABY OF THE WATER-HORSE.)

SUNG BY MARY ROSS,
FROM KILLMALUAG, SKYE, 1897.

Mode 1. *a.* (6-note scale.)

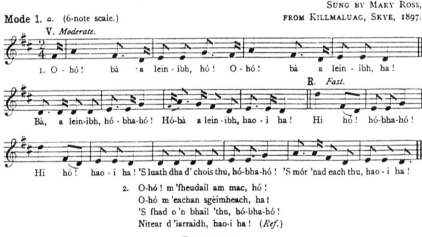

2. O-hó! m 'fheudail am mac, hó!
O-hó m 'eachan sgèimheach, ha!
'S fhad o 'n bhail 'thu, hó-bha-hó!
Nitear d 'iarraidh, haoi-i ha! (*Ref.*)

TRANSLATION.

1. Ohó! sleep thou, child, hó! Ohó! sleep thou, child, ha! Sleep thou, child, hó-bha-hó! Sleep thou, child, haoi-i ha! (*Refrain :* Hi hó! hó-bha-hó! Hi hó! haoi-i ha! Swift art thou of foot, hó-bha-hó, and much art thou of the horse, haoi-i ha!) 2. Ohó, the darling son, hó! Ohó! the comely little horse, ha! Thou art far from home, hó-bha-hó! and wilt be sought for, haoi-i ha! (*Ref.:* Hi ho, etc.)

I have found an apparent variant of this tune attached to the Irish nursery-song, "Chip, chip, my little horse." Even if the words of "Chip, chip," be not a relic of a Gaelic lullaby whose real meaning has been forgotten, the "little water-horse" seems at any rate to have suggested a tune for another nursery-song of a "little horse."—A. G. G.

6.—CAOIDH AN EICH-UISGE.

(LAMENT OF THE WATER-HORSE.)

SUNG BY MARY ROSS,
FROM KILLMALUAG, SKYE, 1897.

Mode 3. *a. b* [with 7th]. (7-note scale.)

1. Och, Och - an 's mi dìr - eadh, Och, Och - an 's mi teàrn - adh: Och, Och - an 's mi dìr - eadh a caoidh na rinn m'fhàg - ail! A dìr - eadh 's a teàrn - adh, A teàrn-adh 's a dìr - eadh; A dìr - eadh 's a teàrn - adh, 'S mi caoidh na rinn m'fhàg - ail. 2. A Mhór thoir a bhruth-ach ort, A Mhór, thoir an gleann ort! A Mhór nach freag-air thu 'n f head? A Mhór - ag bheag nan gamh-na!

TRANSLATION.

1. Alas, as I go climbing! Alas, as I descend! Alas, as I go climbing, and mourning for her who has left me! (*Refrain*: Climbing, descending, etc.) 2. Mór, go up the hill-side! Mór, go down into the glen! Mór, to my shrill cry [*or* whistle] wilt thou not respond? O little Mórag, herding the year-old kine! (R.)

7.—CUMHA AN EICH-UISGE.
(LAMENTATION OF THE WATER-HORSE.)

PENTATONIC.
Mode 4.

SUNG BY KATE MACDIARMID (COTTAR),
MINGINISH, SKYE, 1862.

1. A Mhór - ag dhonn! A   Mhór - ag dhonn! Till gu d 'mhac-an: 'S gheibh thu 'm brad-an breac o 'n loch.

Refrain. A - hó hì. A - hó hì. A - hó hó - an.

A-hó hó - an, A-hó hó - an, A - hó hì. A - hó - hì.   *Fine.*

2. Tha 'n oidhch' an nochd
   Gu fliuch frasach,
   Aig mo mhac-sa ri sgàth cnocain. (R.)

3. Gun teine, gun tuar,
   Gun fhasgadh,
   'S tu sior chonràn. (R.)

4. Mo shean-a chab liath.
   Ri d 'bheul beag baoth.
   'S mi seinn phort duit am Beinn Frochdai. (R.)

TRANSLATION.

1. O brown-haired Morag,* come back to thy little son, and thou shalt get a speckled salmon from the loch. (R.) 2. The night is wet and showery for my son in the shelter of a knoll; (R.) 3. without fire, pale, forlorn, and wailing without cease. (R.) 4. My unsightly old grey mouth, against thy silly little mouth, while I sing dandling songs to thee in Ben Frochdai.† (R.)

The water-horse could assume any form, and, in the likeness of a man, married Morag. On discovering, by the sand on his hair and breast, who he was, she fled from him and their child. The water-horse here sings to the child, hoping to induce Morag to return. *Cf.* the similar air and Gaelic words, contributed by me, in the *Gesto Coll.* (App. p. 20).—F. T.

The story of "the Forsaken Merman," so beautifully presented in English verse by Matthew Arnold, is a favourite one throughout Norway, Sweden and Denmark. It is interesting to find three versions in a Scottish island formerly colonised by Norsemen.

* The diminutive form of "Mór," an ancient female name, commonly Englished "Sarah."

† Between Gesto and Portree, Skye.

For exhaustive notes on the legend *see* "Hind Etin," Child's *English and Scottish Popular Ballads* (large edition). Consult also R. C. Prior's *Ancient Danish Ballads*, vol. iii. (1860), for very interesting versions and notes thereon, under the title "Agnes and the Merman."—L. E. B.

These three "Water-Kelpie" tunes all appear to be Norse in origin. Rhythmically, they are closely akin to two tunes attached to the folk-ballad of "Agnes and the Merman" (Agnete og Havmanden) in *Danmarks Melodier*, and even in the probably modernised form in which those tunes are there given, there are at several points close correspondences in phrase and melody. Though this ballad of "Agnes and the Merman" is the story upon which Matthew Arnold's "Forsaken Merman" is founded, it is an open question whether he was acquainted with the Danish ballad itself. We may have here, in these Water-Kelpie songs, a very interesting Norse survival, and it seems possible to trace the particular form of water-spirit known as a "kelpie" to an origin in that huge uncouth creature of arctic waters, the walrus (literally whale-horse), *rosmar* (*i.e.* sea-horse) in Danish—a sea-beast of whom strange reports would, as we may suppose, be brought home by voyaging Norsemen. The Scandinavian mermen may also, I think, be supposed, on the naturalistic side, to be descended from the walrus genus, just as the Hebridean and north of Scotland mermen and mermaids claim kinship with the "seal-folk" (who also seem to be mixed up with human wearers of seal clothing—Lapps or Finns). It is significant that one of the mermen of the *Kæmpe Viser* collection of ballads—a sea-ogre of great size and strength—is called "*Rosmer* Hafmand" (*hafmand* = merman), and he carries the casket containing the heroine of the story in his mouth—as the most convenient way—and the hero on his back, to the surface of the sea. (The walrus, it may be interpolated, when full grown, attains the length of 18 or 20 feet.) Both *ros* (horse) and *mar* (sea) are old Norse words now obsolete in Danish, though *mar* is still used in compounds in Norway and Shetland, and *russi* is the old Shetland name for a horse.

The legendary pony of the Faroe Isles, which draws whoever touches it down into the sea and drowns him, and possibly also the magic horse of the malevolent "water-man" (in another Danish ballad), which is formed out of "clear water" (a misunderstanding of "water-horse"?) seem to be other forms assumed by the spirit-horse of the sea, after its original embodiment, the walrus, (if here rightly guessed) had become a mere symbol of oil and ivory to its hardy hunters. But both the Water-Kelpie and Agnete's husband are gentler and more lovable forms of *Nycker* than most of the Danish mermen.—A. G. G.

Tales of the sea-man ("bodach mara") are still told in Sutherland.—G. H.

AGNETE OG HAVMANDEN.

FIRST TUNE.

Andantino. FROM *Danmarks Melodier.*

Ag - ne - te, hun stan - der paa Hø - jen-lofts-bro, Strax

R. *f* > >

kom der en Hav - mand, ham gav hun sin Tro. Haa, haa,

haa! Strax kom, etc.

SECOND TUNE.

Allegretto.

R. *f*

Haa, haa, haa !

8.—BA-BÀ, MO LEANABH.

(SLEEP, SLEEP, MY CHILD.)

Mode 5. *a. b.* (7-note scale.)   FROM MRS. BOOG WATSON
PHRYGIAN INFLUENCE.   OF EDINBURGH, 1898.

Rather slow.

Ba - bà mo lean-abh, Ba - bà, ba - bà. Ba - bà mo lean-abh, Ba - bà, ba - bà. Faill

Fine.

ì faill ó, Faill éill o - ro - ho, Gu 'n till na fear - a a dh 'fhalbh thar sàil.

TRANSLATION.

Sleep, my child! Sleep, oh sleep! And may the men return who have gone over the sea!

164

The above variant of a well-known lullaby, with only a few words and the refrain, contributed by me to *Puirt-a-beul*, p. 43, I received from Mrs. Boog Watson of Edinburgh, a true lover of national music, who learned it in her youth when staying near Appin in Argyll, from the late Miss Hughina Maclachlan of Lochaber.—F. T.

In Capt. Fraser's *Collection of Highland Music* there is a variant of this air, under the same title—inferior, however, to this most beautiful and tender melody, which has the character of the rare and singularly expressive Phrygian Mode—a mode whose minor 2nd (like a descending leading-note), lends it a peculiar pathos. *Cf.* "Caoidh Màthar" and others in this present collection.—A. G. G.

9.—NA CREID IAD.

(BELIEVE THEM NOT.)

PENTATONIC.
Mode 3.
Moderate.

LEARNT IN INFANCY, AT UIGNISH, SKYE, AND HEARD AT BRACADALE MANSE, 1860.—F. T.

Na creid iad, a Ghaoil do Mhàth-ar! Na creid iad gu 'm fag-ainn thu. Ma dh' fhalbh-as mi 'n diu, Thig mi 'm màir-each, 'S na creid iad gu 'm fag-ainn thu!

TRANSLATION.

Believe them not, thou darling of thy mother! Believe not that I would forsake thee! If I go away to-day, I shall return to-morrow! Oh, believe not that I would leave thee!

10.—AM FACA TU 'N GOBHA?

(HAST THOU SEEN THE SMITH?)

FRAGMENT HEARD AT BRACADALE MANSE, SKYE, 1861.—F. T.

Mode 3. *a* (6-note scale.)
Slow.

Am fac-a tu 'n Gobh'? Chall eil-ibh ho ro ho. No 'm fac-a tu 'n Gobh-a? Chall o ho ro i. Cha teid mi a Mhuil-e; Cha dean mi ann

165

fuir - each, Gus an ais - ig mi uil - e Mo ghrunn - an beag spréidh.

TRANSLATION.

Hast thou seen the smith? etc. I am not going to Mull, nor will settle there, till I shall have ferried over my little lot of cattle.

11.—THA SÌOR CHOINEADH AM BEINN-DÓRAIN.

(THERE IS CONSTANT WAILING IN BEN DORAN.)

SUNG BY MRS. H. M'KENZIE,
DUNVEGAN, SKYE, 1862.

Mode 3. *a. b.* [with ♭7th]. (7-note scale.)

Slow.

Tha sìor chóin - eadh am Beinn - Dór - ain, Tha gal is cóin - eadh 's a'

bheinn ud thall. Tha glaodh mo laoigh 's a' bheinn, 's a' bheinn ; Tha

glaodh mo laoigh 's a' bheinn ud thall ; Tha glaodh mo laoigh 's a'

Fine.

bheinn, 's a' bheinn, tha sìor eigh - each 's a' bheinn ud thall.

TRANSLATION.

There is constant wailing in Ben Doran ;[*] weeping and wailing are in yonder hill [repeat]. The voice of my darling is on the mountain, the mountain ; the voice of my darling is on yonder mountain ; the voice of my darling is on the mountain, the mountain ; and constant crying over there.

For a similar air contributed by me, with a third verse, see *Puirt-a-beul*, p. 46. The word "Cóineadh" is written as pronounced in Skye.—F. T.

[*] The reference is to what is known to shepherds and others who are often out at night as *a 'ghaoir-uisge, a'ghairm-uisge*, a loud continuous murmuring sound, like the cry of a child in pain. It is very eerie in its rise and fall, and may last for ten minutes. It is a natural phenomenon, and is a forerunner of wind and rain. "Beindouran in Glenorchy . . . emits this noise in a most striking manner." I have given other instances in *Memoirs of a Highland Gentleman* (J. & A. Constable, Edin., 1905). The *d* properly belongs to the *beinn*, older *benn, bend*; hence *bend-órain* : *cf.* Oran-more, Galway, now Uarán mór. Cognate is

12.—AN CUBHRACHAN.

(THE SWEET LITTLE ONE.)

Mode 3. *a. b* [with ?7th]. (7-note scale.)
MIXOLYDIAN INFLUENCE.

SUNG BY JANET ANDERSON (NURSE), CONTIN MANSE, ROSS-SHIRE, 1870.

Rather slow.

1. Och, Och, nan Och ! mar tha mi fhéin ! Mar tha mi fhéin, mar tha mi fhéin ! Och.

Och, nan Och ! mar tha mi fhéin ! 'S mo shùil an déidh mo Chùbhr - ach - an !

2. Shiubhail mi'n gleann, o cheann gu ceann,
O cheann gu ceann, o cheann gu ceann.
Shiubhail min 'n gleann, o cheann gu ceann,
Ach, O ! cha d'fhuair mi'n Cùbhrachan.

3. Fhuair mi lorg an dobhrain duinn, etc.

4. Fhuair mi lorg an eal' air an t-snàmh, etc.

5. Fhuair mi lorg an laoigh-bhric, dheirg, etc.

TRANSLATION.

1. (and Ch.) Alas, alas ! In what grief am I,
In what grief am I, in what grief am I,
Alas, alas ! In what grief am I,
Searching for my Cubhrachan.

2. I traversed the glen from end to end ; etc.
But oh, found not the Cubhrachan.

3. I found the track of the brown otter, etc.
But oh.

4. I found the trace of the swimming swan, etc.
But oh.

5. I found the track of the spotted red fawn ; etc.
But oh.

The Cubhrachan is carried away by the fairies, and his sorrowing mother seeks him in vain. There is a translation of this song in *Lyra Celtica*, p. 218, and a version of the Gaelic words in the *Duanaire*, p. 94. *Cf.* "An Cóineachen" in *Minstrelsy of the Scottish Highlands*, and *Celtic Lyre*, No. 56. The name is derived from the word "Cùbhraidh," fragrant, sweet.—F. T.

There is a strong likeness between this tune and that of an "Irish Lullaby," noted by Dr. W. P. Joyce in 1854 from a Limerick singer (see *Petrie Coll.* 1855). The latter tune, with Dr. Sigerson's translation of the original words, is in Moffat's *Minstrelsy of Ireland*, and it also appears in very slightly varied form, with words by A. P. Graves, in Stanford's *Songs of Old Ireland*. The Gaelic air is much like one very commonly used in England by children in their singing-games : "Here come three Dukes," "Tripping up the Green Grass," "Poor Mary is a-weeping," etc.—L. E. B.

Welsh *oer* = cold. The Sutherland *uar*, applied to a scooped hollow with water and gravel coming down in a spate. is from the same root. In the place-name the older form of the vowel has been retained. The name is well descriptive of a mountain where spates come on suddenly, as I once experienced. —G. H.

13.—DEAN CADALAN.

(SLEEP THOU AWHILE.)

PENTATONIC.
Mode 4.

SUNG BY MARY ROSS,
FROM KILLMALUAG, ISLE OF SKYE, AT OBAN, 1900.

Rather slow.

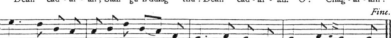

Dean cad - al - an; Slàn gu 'n dùisg thu! Dean cad - al - an. O! Chag - ar - ain!

Fine.

'S è b 'fhaid-e leam, Gun a bhi dlùth dhuit, Dean cad - al - an, Slàn gu 'n dùisg thu!

TRANSLATION.

Sleep for a while and be well on awaking! Sleep a while, thou little dear! Much would it grieve me not to be near thee. Sleep for a while, and awake thou well!

14.—THA NA FEIDH, O-HO.

(THE DEER ARE THERE, O-HO!)

Mode 1. *a.* (6-note scale.)

SUNG BY MARY ROSS,
FROM KILLMALUAG, SKYE, 1908.

Slow. V.

1. Tha na féidh, o - ho! B 'è na féidh iàd! Tha na féidh

o - ho! Air a' Bheinn àrd. All - ail - a hó hó - an!

All - ail - a hó ho! All - ail - a hó, hó - an. O hó - an ó.

Fine.

2. Leig an cù riutha;
   Cuir an cù unnt';
   Leig an cù riutha;
   An cù dona dall.
        All-ail-a hó, etc.

TRANSLATION.

1. The deer are there, O-ho! The deer—certainly they are [*or* how wonderful they are]. The deer are yonder, O-ho! high up the Ben. (*Refrain*: All-ail-a, etc.) 2. Slip the dog after them : set the dog on, send the dog after them—the dog useless and blind (Refrain).

The interchange of C♯ and C♮ in bars 5 and 6 is very characteristic.—J. A. F. M.

15.—'S MILIS MORAG.

(SWEET IS MORAG.)

SUNG BY MARY ROSS,
FROM KILLMALUAG, SKYE, AT OBAN, 1900.

Mode 3. *b.* (6-note scale.)
Rather slow.
Fine.

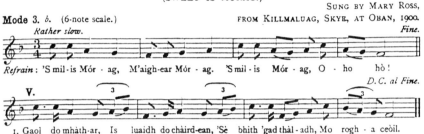

Refrain: 'S mil-is Mór - ag, M'aigh-ear Mór - ag. 'S mil - is Mór - ag, O - ho hò !

D.C. al Fine.

1. Gaol do mhàth-ar, Is luaidh do chàird-ean, 'Se bhith 'gad thàl-adh, Mo rogh - a ceòil.

2. M 'anam fhéin thu,
Ogha an fhidhleir,
'S gur beag an t-ioghnadh
Thu bhith'g a chòir.

TRANSLATION.

(*Refrain*: Morag is sweet, and my joy is Morag.) 1. Thy mother's darling, dear to thy kindred, my choice of music is to be lulling thee. (Refrain.) 2. My own soul art thou, grand-child of the violinist, and little cause is there for wonder that thou shouldest resemble him. (Refrain.)

A tune formed on the same five notes as "Slàn gu 'n tig Aonachan," No. 16 in this collection. A song with a similar refrain is "Gur milis Mórag," in Mrs. Kennedy Fraser's *Songs of the Hebrides.*—A. G. G.

16.—SLÀN GU 'N TIG AONACHAN.

(BE IT WELL WITH AONACHAN.)

SUNG BY OIGHRIG ROSS,
BRACADALE, SKYE, 1861.

Mode 3. *b.* (6-note scale.)

Slow March.

Slàn gu 'n tig Aon-ach-an, Slàn gu 'n tig O ! Slàn gu 'n tig Aon-ach-an, Slàn gu 'n tig O !

Slàn gu 'n tig Aon-ach-an, Slàn gu 'n tig   O !   Slàn gu 'n tig, slàn gu 'n ruig, Slàn gu 'n tig   O !

TRANSLATION.

Be it well with Aonachan, well be he, O ! [*thrice*].   Well be he, well may he arrive, well be he, O !

This tune was chanted at funerals in the olden time, when no harp or bag-pipe was obtainable; and might also be heard in our own day as a lullaby.   The meaning of Aonachan is "the solitary," the one who is alone.—F. T.

Cf. the preceding tune " 'S milis Mórag" in the same limited five-note range.— A. G. G.

Cf. this air with the various forms of "Crodh Chailein" ("Colin's Cattle"), good examples of which are in the *Celtic Lyre,* and in the *Killin Coll.* and *Gesto Coll.*   In the latter there are, besides three variants called "Crodh Chailein," also variants on p. 35, and Appendix, p. 28, entitled "an original Gaelic air" and "An Siùdagan Iomlan, the universal lullaby."   I have a phonographed air to "Crodh Chailein" (sung frequently as a lullaby), from Ross-shire.   This is very similar to Miss Tolmie's tune.   The air appears as "O can ye sew cushions?" in the *Scots Musical Museum,* to which it was contributed by Burns.   Stenhouse quotes an additional Lowland-Scottish lullaby verse, and observes that Burns has left us no hints respecting the history of the song.

A very remarkable likeness exists between several forms of this Gaelic air and an old Swiss May Day carol, sung in the Canton of Zurich with precisely the same customs and decorations as those formerly usual in England.   The Swiss carol-words also present striking parallels with our May and Christmas carols and wassail songs.   The traditional chant is given below, without its repetitions, which merely show one or two immaterial variations.—L. E. B.

SWISS MAY DAY CAROL.

DAS ALTE SECHSELÄUTENLIED.

NOTED BEFORE 1849,

FROM *Schweizerisches Archiv für Volkskunde,* 11TH SERIES, 1907.

17.—'MHNÀTHAN A'GHLINNE SO!

(YE WOMEN OF THIS GLEN.)

Mode 3. a. b [with ♭7th]. (7-note scale.)
MIXOLYDIAN INFLUENCE.

As sung in the Nursery, at Contin Manse, Ross-shire, 1870.

Slow march.

'Mhnathan, etc.

2. Mharbh 'ad am buachaille [*thrice*].
Bha 'cuallach na spréidhe.

TRANSLATION.

1. O ye women of this glen [*thrice*], is it not time for you to rise? 'Tis I was up very early [*thrice*], for your sake did I rise!

2. O ye women of this glen [*thrice*], etc. They have slain the cowherd [*thrice*], who was tending the kine.

This was a favourite lullaby, and, with "Griogal Cridhe" in this collection, known in every Highland home. It is commemorative of the terrors of a cattle-raid. Two pibrochs were composed on the same tune; one in remembrance of the feud between the Campbells of Breadalbane and the Sinclairs of Caithness in 1677; the other, of the horrid act of treachery committed in Glencoe, 1692. For one version *see* the *Killin Collection of Highland Music*, by Charles Stewart.—F. T.

171

This air (known as "Lord Breadalbane's March") is in the *Inverness Collection of Highland Pibrochs*, and in many other collections of Highland songs and music. *Cf.* "Mhuinntir a' Ghlinne so." ("Ye Men of the Glen") in *A Choisir-Chiuil.* Usually the 7th is omitted altogether, or, if present, is unflattened. I have noted a version with these same words in Inverness-shire; this has no 7th. The flat 7th of Miss Tolmie's tune is interesting and apparently unusual.—L. E. B.

18.—SIUD A LEINIBH.

(ROCK THEE, O CHILD!)

Mode 3. *b.* (6-note scale.)

Slow.

SUNG BY MARY ROSS, FROM KILLMALUAG, SKYE, 1900.

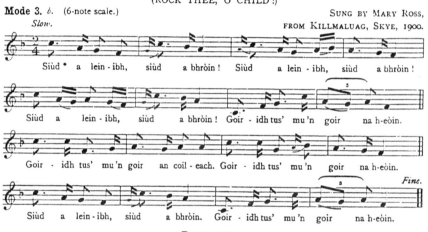

Siùd* a lein - ibh, siùd a bh ròin! Siùd a lein - ibh, siùd a bh ròin!

Siùd a lein - ibh, siùd a bh ròin! Goir - idh tus' mu 'n goir na h-eòin.

Goir - idh tus' mu 'n goir an coil - each. Goir - idh tus' mu 'n goir na h-eòin.

Siùd a lein - ibh, siùd a bh ròin. Goir - idh tus' mu 'n goir na h-eòin. *Fine.*

TRANSLATION.

Rock thee, O child! Rock to sleep, thou darling! Ere the birds begin to chirp thou wilt call. Thou wilt cry ere the cock will crow. Thou wilt cry ere the birds will sing. Rock thee, O child, etc.

There is a considerable resemblance between this tune and that of an old Danish lullaby, four different forms of which are given in *Bφrnenes Musik*—a collection of Danish nursery-songs and singing-games. The rhythm and some of the phrases are almost identical with those of two of these Danish versions, and as "Siùd a Leinibh" does not seem to me to be Gaelic in character, it may perhaps be an old Norse lullaby tune. (Less than 200 years ago a number of old Norse ballads still existed in Shetland, and it seems quite likely that some similar relics of Norse occupation may have been preserved further south, in the Hebrides.)—A. G. G.

* Alternative: "Siuthad" or "Siuth'd."

VISSE LULLE, MIT LILLE BARN.

Andante.

FROM *Bφrnenes Musik.*

Vis - se lulle, mit lil - le Barn

MODER SPINDER GARN.

SECOND VERSION OF TUNE.

Andante.

Ibid.

Sov, sov, mit Barn

Snur, snur, snur!

19.—AN CÙ BÀN.

(THE WHITE DOG.)

Mode 3. *a. b* [with 7th].
MIXOLYDIAN INFLUENCE.

SUNG BY MARY ROSS,
FROM KILLMALUAG, SKYE, 1899.

Rather slow.

R.

V.

Fine.

"Obh - an ! òbh - an !" ars' an Cù Bàn. 1. "Mis' air an air - igh !" ars' an Cù Bàn.

2. "Mharbh am bròn ini," ars' an Cù Bàn,
3. " A 'gleidheil a chàise," ars' an Cù Bàn.

TRANSLATION.

(*Refrain*: "Oh, oh !" said the white dog.) 1. " At the sheiling am I." said the white dog. 2. "Sorrow has killed me," said the white dog, 3. " While guarding the cheese," said the white dog.

173

20.—ORAN TALAIDH NA MNA-SIDHE.

PENTATONIC. (THE LULLABY OF THE FAIRY-WOMAN.)

Mode 2.
Not too slow.

SUNG BY MR. NEIL MACLEOD, GAELIC BARD, 1908.

1. "'Sè mo lean-abh ming-il-is-each,* maing-il-is-each, 'Bual-adh nan each, 'glac nan lùir-each; Nan each crùidh-each, 's nan each snag-ach.† Mo lean-abh beag!

2. 'S truagh nach fhaic-inn fhéin do bhuail-e, Gu h-àrd, àrd air uachd-ar sléibh-e; Còt-a caol cait-ein-each uain-e, Mu d' dhà ghual-ainn ghil is léin-e. Mo lean-abh beag!

3. 'S truagh nach fhaic-inn fhéin do sheis-reach; Fir 'na déidh; Mnài-còmh-dhail a tigh 'nn dhach-aidh, 'S na Cat-an-aich a' cur shìl."

4. "O mhìl-idh bhog! O, mhìl-idh bhog, O, mhìl-idh bhog! Mo bhrù a rug; Mo chioch a shluig, Mo ghlùn a thog!

5. 'Sè mo lean-abh m'ult-ach iubh-air, sult-mhor reamh-ar, mo luach-air bhog! M'fheòil is m'uibh-ean a ni bhruidh-eann. Bha thu fo mo chrios an uir-idh; Lus an tor-aidh. 'S bidh tu 'm bliadh-na

† "Snagach" here signifies the clapping together of spirited horses' feet. "Snag" = a smart tap, "snagarr(a)" = active, lively, alert.—N. M.

174

(Mode changes from 2 to 3.)

* *Mingiliseach* is from a side form of the root in *meann*, kid, whence the diminutive *minnein*, a small kid ; the ending seems founded on *leis* or *slios*. Hence *minniriseach*, save that the sound is influenced by the following *maingiliseach*, from *mang-leis-ach*. The *i* before the *l* is a parasitic vowel.—G. H.

TRANSLATION.

[*Fairy sings*] " 1. Behold my child, limbed like the kid and fawn, smiting the horses, seizing the accoutrements of the shod horses, the spirited steeds. My little child ! 2. Oh, that I could see thy cattle-fold, high up on the mountain-side : a green, shaggy jacket about thy two white shoulders, with a linen shirt. My little child ! 3. Oh, that I could behold thy team of horses : men following them : serving-women returning home, and the Catanaich † sowing the corn." [*His mother sings*] " 4. O tender hero [*sing thrice*] whom my womb did bring forth, who didst swallow from my breast, who on my knee wast reared. 5. My child it is, my armful of yew [bows and arrows], merry and plump, my bulrush, my flesh and eggs, that will soon be speaking. Last year thou wast beneath my girdle, plant of fertility ! and this year, fair and playful on my shoulder, thou wilt be going round the homestead. 6. (Obh, i-rinn obh-o !) Oh ! let me not hear of thy being wounded. (Obh, etc.) Grey do thou become duly. (Obh, etc.) May

† *i.e.* men of the Clan Chattan, or here possibly Cattanachs.

thy nose grow sharp [with advancing age], (Obh, etc.) ere the close of thy day ! 7. (Obh i-rinn obh-inn thu !),
Oh ! not of Clan Kenneth [Mackenzies,] art thou ! ('Bh i-rinn, etc.) Oh ! not of Clan Conn [Macdonalds,].
('Bh i-rinn, etc.) Descendant of a race more esteemed ; that of the Clan Leòd [Macleods,] of swords
and armour, whose fathers' native land was Lochlann [Scandinavia]."

The singer of this ancient fragment, Mr. Neil Macleod, a Gaelic bard of Skye, and author of *Clàrsach an Doire* (*Harp of the Grove*), the fourth edition of which is dated 1909, is a son of Donald Macleod, commonly known as the "Skye Bard" ("Am Bard Sgitheanach"). Donald, of whom there is an account in Mackenzie's *Beauties of Gaelic Poetry* under the head "Am Bard Sgiathanach" (*sic*), was born about the year 1785, and died at the age of 87. His son Neil was born on his father's croft, Glendale, in the parish of Duirinish, to which Dunvegan belongs. From his father he learnt the words given above ; unfortunately the elder bard was unable to recover all the verses of the song, which even in his day was remembered by but a few old people, and in incomplete form. The music of the lullaby, which I believe had never before been recorded, was carefully noted by me from the singing of Mr. Neil Macleod, whose many patient repetitions alone made it possible to fix it correctly. The following is the legend attaching to the song :

One day in the island of Skye, many centuries ago, a woman of wonderful aspect— in point of fact a fairy or "banshee"—appeared suddenly at the door of Dunvegan, the castle of Macleod of Macleod. She entered the castle without invitation, and went straight into the room where the infant heir lay asleep in his cradle. Taking him in her arms, she sang a song, of which the foregoing verses are only a fragment. Then, laying him down, she passed out of the castle, and vanished over the moor as mysteriously as she had come. Her fairy lullaby was ever after regarded as a charm to protect the young heir of Macleod from every evil. No woman was allowed to be his nurse who could not sing it over him. But in course of time the meanings of certain words and expressions became obscure ; it must be at least a hundred years since a nurse to Macleod's heir used the lullaby, literally as an "incantation," and, as we have seen, the song is nearly unknown to-day. However, in *Waifs and Strays of Celtic Tradition* (vol. v. p. 141) there is a variant of the words, given by Campbell of Islay to the editor, Rev. J. G. Campbell of Tiree, in 1871. In that version the mother and the fairy sing alternately over the child, whereas, in Mr. Macleod's, the mother seems only to sing at the point indicated. Another variant of the words is in *Puirt mo Sheanamhar*, edited by T. D. M'Donald.—F. T.

For very suggestive matter in connection with lullabies as charms consult *La Musique et la Magie*, by Dr. Jules Combarieu (Picard et Fils, Paris, 1909). Dr. Combarieu traces the use of magical lullabies to Egyptian papyri and ancient Greek references. He also finds that nonsense refrains were used *magically* earlier than *rhythmically*.

In a version of this "Lullaby of the Fairy Woman," published on p. 108 of the Rev. J. Macdougall's *Folk Tales and Fairy Lore* (Edinburgh, 1910), and almost identical with Mr. Macleod's version, an attempt has been made to restore the original meaning of the refrain by writing it "O bheirinn o bho ... O bheirinn o bhinn thu," which is translated, "O I'd snatch thee from cow, ... O I'd snatch thee from doom." Possibly many of the nonsense refrains so common in Gaelic songs had originally as much meaning as the "Sint thugaibh i, etc." of No. 64 in this collection, of which an explanation has been attempted; but Miss Tolmie assures me that for her and for the singers from whom she learned her songs all sense of meaning in the words has been entirely lost, the syllables being regarded as of purely rhythmical value. In Mr. Macdougall's version the 2nd line of v. 3 runs "Fir 'ga freasdal 'n àm an fheasgair" ("And the men tend it, at evening beam") in place of Mr. Macleod's "Fir na dèidh" ("Men following them"). As the phrasing of the music suggests that a bar has been omitted at this point, it seems probable that the longer line supplies the correct number of syllables.—L. E. B.

21.—'PHIUTHRAG NAM PIUTHAR.

(LITTLE SISTER OF SISTERS.)

Mode 2. *a. b.* (7-note scale.)

FROM THE NOTATION OF THE LATE REV. JOHN MACDONALD OF HARRIS.

Slow.

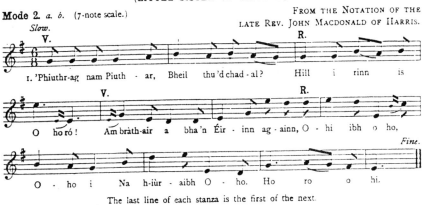

1. 'Phiuthr-ag nam Piuth - ar, Bheil thu'd chad-al? Hill i rinn is O ho ró! Am bràth-air a bha 'n Éir - inn ag-ainn, O - hi ibh o ho, O - ho i Na h-iùr - aibh O - ho. Ho ro o hi.

Fine.

The last line of each stanza is the first of the next.

TRANSLATION.

1. Little sister, dearest of sisters, art thou sleeping? (Hill i, etc.). 2. The brother whom we had in Ireland (O hi, etc.), 3. they were bearing yesterday on staves. 4. I was there unknown to them; 5. now on the ground, then on horse-back, 6. and again for a while enfolded in silk.

The air of this lullaby was given many years ago by the late Rev. John Macdonald, minister of Harris, to the late Miss Macdonald, Rodel, in Harris, from whose cousin I received it in remembrance of her. With the permission of the Rev. Archibald Macdonald of Kiltarlity, I have quoted from the *Transactions of the Gaelic Society of Inverness* a few lines and the refrain to go with the tune.—F. T.

From the few lines quoted, this lullaby would seem to be a version of the "Fairy Plaint" ("Ceòl Brutha") given in Mrs. Kennedy Fraser's *Songs of the Hebrides* to another tune—a song which is the plaint of a woman who has been spirited from her home by fairies, and returns invisible to hold converse with her "little sister of sisters."—A. G. G.

22.—BUAIN NA RAINICH.
(CUTTING THE BRACKEN.)

PENTATONIC.
Mode 4.

AN EARLY MEMORY
FROM UIGNISH, SKYE.—F. T.

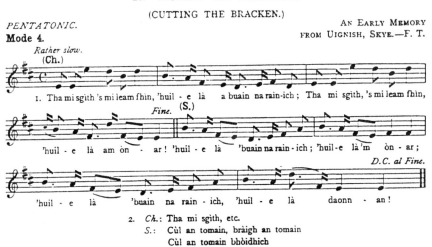

2. *Ch.*: Tha mi sgìth, etc.
   S.: Cùl an tomain, bràigh an tomain
   Cùl an tomain bhòidhich
   Cùl an tomain, bràigh an tomain
   'huile la 'm ònar. (Ch.)

TRANSLATION.

1. *Chorus*: I am weary all alone, the whole day, cutting the bracken; I am weary all alone, alone all the day! *Solo*: All the day, cutting the bracken, all the day alone! All the day, etc., all the day for ever. 2. *Chorus*: I am weary, etc. *Solo*: Behind the knoll, upon the knoll, behind the pretty knoll; behind the knoll, upon the knoll, all the day alone! (Ch.)

A maiden had a fairy lover who used to help her when cutting bracken or drying peats on the moor. Her brothers having suspected that she must be receiving fairy assistance, set a watch to observe her, and, on finding that their suspicions were confirmed, carried their sister away to a distant part of the country, and the fairy saw her no more; but he was often heard lamenting her absence, behind the pretty knoll wherein was his abode. The above is a very ancient lullaby, universally known throughout the Highlands. For another version see *Songs of the Hebrides*, edited by Mrs. Kennedy Fraser.—F. T.

Cf. for general design, the beautiful lowland air, "Ca' the Yowes to the Knowes." —J. A. F. M.

For very similar copies of this air see *The Thistle*, p. 99, and also the *Celtic Lyre*, No. 50, "Eilidh Bhan."—A. G. G.

NURSE'S SONGS.

23.—HO! MHÓRAG BHEAG!

(HO! LITTLE MORAG!)

SUNG BY MARY ROSS,
FROM KILLMALUAG, SKYE, 1900.

Mode 3. *a.* (6-note scale.)

Moderate.

Fine.

1. Hó Mhór-ag bheag! O-hao Mhór-ag bheag! O hó Mhór-ag bheag! Rach-ainn ead-ar thu 's a' chreig!

2. Hó Mhórag a ghaoil
Rachainn eadar thu 's a' ghaoith.

3. Hó Mhórag a luaidh
Rachainn eadar thu 's a' fuachd.

TRANSLATION.

1. Ho! little Morag! I would go between thee and the rock! 2. Ho! Morag, my love, I would go between thee and the storm. 3. Ho! Morag, thou dear, I would go between thee and the cold.

24.—'S AIGHEARACH MI.

(JOYFUL AM I.)

SUNG BY MARY ROSS,
FROM KILLMALUAG, SKYE, 1908.

Mode 1. *a.* (6-note scale.)

Moderate.

D.C. Chorus al Fine.

(Ch.)

Fine. (S.)

'S aigh-ear-ach mi, 's mo ghill' air mo ghual-ainn; 1. Og-an-ach fin-ealt a dh'fhin-e nan uais-lean.

2. Cha leig mi do neach thu ni buill' ort a bhualadh. (Ch.)

[By a foster-mother.]

179

TRANSLATION.

(*Chorus*: Joyful am I, with my boy on my shoulder.) 1. Handsome youth of the race of the nobles. (*Chorus*: Joyful am I, etc.) 2. I will give thee to none who may strike thee a blow. (Ch.)

I have noted a longer air, of which this is perhaps a variant, in Inverness-shire, to "Blind Allan's" (Alan Dall's) words in praise of whiskey, "Duanag Do'n Uisge-Bheatha." Both are very characteristic of a lively West Highland type of tune.—L. E. B.

25.—AN TÉID THU BHUAIN MHAORAICH?

(WILT THOU GO AND GATHER SHELL-FISH?)

Mode 4. *a. b.*
DORIAN INFLUENCE.

SUNG BY MARY ROSS, FROM KILLMALUAG, SKYE.
EDINBURGH, 1908.

TRANSLATION.

Wilt thou go and gather shell-fish? Wilt thou go and gather limpets by the Channel-of-the-Aird? Thou darling—thy mother's darling! Wilt thou go and gather limpets? etc.

26.—'FAC THU NA FÉIDH?

(HAST THOU SEEN THE DEER?)

SUNG IN THE NURSERY
AT BRACADALE MANSE, SKYE, 1861.

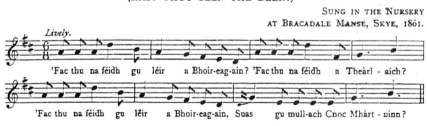

Ruidh - lidh Boir-eag-an, danns - aidh Boir-eag-an ; Ruidh - lidh Boir-eag-an, Thearl - aich !

Ar - an is ìm dhomh fhin 's do Bhoir-eag-an. Suas gu mull-ach Cnoc-Mhàrt - uinn.

TRANSLATION.

Hast thou seen the deer all together, O Boireagan? Has thou seen them, Charlie? Hast thou, etc. Up by the top of Knock Martin. Boireagan will reel, and Boireagan will dance, Boireagan will reel, O Charlie! Bread and butter for me and Boireagan, up to the top of Knock Martin.

A spirited tune formed on almost the same rhythmical pattern as the old air, "The Hemp-dresser" ("The De'il's awa wi' the Exciseman"), claimed by both Scotland and Wales. The first four bars after the double bar are almost identical with the old Lancashire "Cross-Morris" tune, but the air generally has a strong resemblance to "Over the Water to Charlie." I feel some doubt whether the tune be of Gaelic origin. If G is regarded as the tonic, the tune is in Mode 3. a. *See* note to "Till an Crodh," No. 28 in this collection.—A. G. G.

27.—TOGAIBH È, TOGAIBH È.

(REAR YE HIM, REAR YE HIM.)

Mode 2. *a.* (6-note scale.)   SUNG BY MARY ROSS, FROM KILLMALUAG, SKYE.

Moderate.   EDINBURGH, 1900.

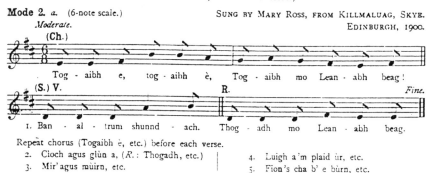

(Ch.)

   Tog - aibh   e,   tog - aibh   è,   Tog - aibh   mo   Lean - abh   beag !

(S.) V.   **R.**   *Fine.*

1. Ban - al - trum shunnd - ach.   Thog - adh   mo   Lean - abh   beag.

Repeat chorus (Togaibh è, etc.) before each verse.

2. Cioch agus glùn a, (*R.*: Thogadh, etc.)   4. Luigh a 'm plaid ùr, etc.
3. Mir' agus mùirn, etc.   5. Fion 's cha b' e bùrn, etc.

TRANSLATION.

(*Chorus*: Rear ye him, rear ye him, rear ye my little child.) 1. A nurse in good health (*R.*: to rear my little babe.) 2. A bosom and knee, to rear (etc.). 3. With joy and love (etc.). 4. To lie in a blanket quite new (etc.). 5. And no water but wine (etc.).

Cf. "Till an Crodh," and "Dh'fhalbh an -triùir," Nos. 28 and 29 in this collection.—F. T.

This is one of the Celtic rhythms absolutely foreign to English folk-song, and imitated with difficulty in Lowland-Scottish verses written to such tunes. It illustrates the tendency of Gaelic tunes to end not only on a weak accent, but on the weakest part of the bar. The character of many of such tunes has been entirely destroyed in printed collections by depriving them of this soft terminal accent in order to fit them to the poetical system and forms of another language—English or Scottish—though the former is the more unbending of the two. On the other hand, an expletive and too frequent "O" at the end of the line—as in Tannahill's song to the air, "Mòr Nighean a' Ghiobarlain," beginning "Blythe was the time when he fee'd with my father *O*"— seems a poor evasion of the difficulty of fitting words to such a phrase as this— peculiarly characteristic of Gaelic song:

—a rhythm requiring for *English* verses a supply of triple rhymes on the pattern of the word "wilderness"!—A. G. G.

28.—TILL AN CRODH, DHONNACHAIDH!

(TURN THE CATTLE, DUNCAN.)

Mode 3. *a. b* [with ♭7th]. *See Note.*

SUNG IN THE NURSERY
AT BRACADALE MANSE, SKYE, 1861.

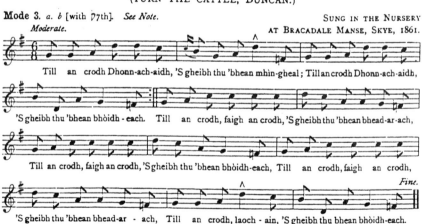

Till an crodh Dhonn-ach-aidh, 'S gheibh thu 'bhean mhìn-gheal; Till an crodh Dhonn-ach-aidh,

'S gheibh thu 'bhean bhòidh-each. Till an crodh, faigh an crodh, 'S gheibh thu 'bhean bhead-ar-ach,

Till an crodh, faigh an crodh, 'S gheibh thu 'bhean bhòidh-each, Till an crodh, faigh an crodh,

'S gheibh thu 'bhean bhead-ar - ach, Till an crodh, laoch - ain, 'S gheibh thu bhean bhòidh-each.

Turn the cattle, Duncan, and thou shalt get the woman soft and fair. Turn the cattle, Duncan, and the lovely woman shall be thine. Turn the cattle, find the cattle, and thou shalt have the charming woman. Turn the cattle, my fine fellow, and thou shalt get a lovely bride.

This sounds like a bagpipe-tune, and like many of these pipe-tunes, *e.g.* "Gillie-Callum," appears to be constructed upon a pair of chords corresponding to the major common chords of F and G. If it has a place at all in the modal system of my preface, the last note cannot be regarded as the tonic, which seems to be G. It seems possible that by analogy with the Gaelic system of poetry, we may solve some questions of tonality with regard to certain tunes which end with an unaccented note. In Gaelic poetry such words as "*cra*dle" and "*la*bour" would rhyme, the unaccented syllable being ignored. And in certain tunes possibly the same principle may unconsciously be applied, and the last *accented* note be treated as the tonic, and the unaccented one following it counted a negligible note, free to rise or fall at the fancy of the singer. Such a principle—or habit—would, perhaps, solve the problem of such tunes as "Till an Crodh" and "Fac thu na Féidh."—A. G. G.

For a distinct major march tune to the same title see *Gesto Coll.*—L. E. B.

29.—DH'FHALBH AN TRIÙIR MHAIGHDINNEAN (i.).

(THE THREE MAIDENS HAVE GONE AWAY.)

PENTATONIC.

Mode 4.

SUNG IN THE NURSERY
AT BRACADALE MANSE, SKYE, 1861.

Moderate.

1. Dh'fhalbh an triùir Mhaigh-dinn-ean, Dh'fhalbh an triùir Mhaigh-dinn-ean,

Fine.

Dh'fhalbh an triùir Mhaigh-dinn-ean, Leis an triùir Shaighd-ear-an.

29.—DH'FHALBH AN TRIÙIR MHAIGHDINNEAN (ii.).

(THE THREE MAIDENS HAVE GONE AWAY.)

SUNG BY MARY ROSS,
FROM KILLMALUAG, SKYE, 1900.

Mode 3. *a. b.* [with 7th].

Slow.

1. Dh'fhalbh an triùir Mhaigh-dinn-ean, Dh'fhalbh an triùir Mhaigh - dinn-ean,

183

Dh'fhalbh an triùir Mhaigh-dinn-ean, Leis an triùir Shaigh-dear-an.

2. Dh'fhalbh an triùir nigheanagan [*thrice*] | 3. Dh'fhalbh an triùir ghruagaichean [*thrice*]
Leis an triùir chìbeirean. | Leis an triùir bhuachaillean.

4. Dh'fhalbh na trì "Màirinean" [*thrice*]
Leis na trì àilleagain.

TRANSLATION.

1. The three maidens have gone away [*thrice*] with the three soldiers. 2. The three girls have gone away with the three shepherds. 3. The three young women have gone away with the three herdsmen. 4. The three, named Mary, have gone away with the three most beautiful.

The opening phrase and position of the flat 7th in the second version is very characteristic of West Highland airs. I have noted several similar tunes, one to Rob Donn Mackay's "Lament" on Isabel Mackay.—L. E. B.

This particular flat 7th, which has a peculiar and special effect of extra flatness, recognisable by the ear, and not shared by the other minor intervals of the Gaelic modes, always corresponds, according to my reckoning, to the occasional E♭ of the modal system stated in my preface. *E.g.* though the tune above appears at first sight to be in Mode 1, it will be noted that its third degree is too essential to the tune to be regarded as the imported 3rd of that mode, but must be considered as belonging to the original pentatonic framework. The tune is, therefore (with several others of the same type in this collection), assigned to Mode 3, with its native major 3rd and imported flattened 7th.—A. G. G.

30.—MAOLRUAINIDH GHLINNEACHAIN.

(MAOLRUAINI GHLINNEACHAIN.)

Mode 4. a. (6-note scale.)

Moderate.

SUNG IN THE NURSERY
AT BRACADALE MANSE, SKYE, 1861.

1. Hù a-hó, Maol ruain-idh Ghlinn-each-ain. Hì a-hó, Maol-ruain-idh!

Dh'fhalbh do Mhàth-air, 's thug i'm fir-each oirr'. Hù a-hó, Maol-ruain-idh!

184

2. Dh' fhalbh do mhàthair, 's thug i 'm fireach oirr',
   Hì a-hó ! Maolruainidh !
   'S thug i 'm balg 'san robh do chuid mine leath'.
   Hù a-hó ! Maolruainidh !

3.* 'S thug i 'n curasan 'san robh do chuid ime leath'.

4. 'S na bu tig an aon là thilleas i.

* The second line of each verse forms the first of the succeeding stanza. The new second line only is printed.—F. T.

TRANSLATION.

1. Hu-a-ho ! Maolruaini Ghlinneachain ! (*Refrain* : Hì a-hó, etc.) Thy mother has gone away and betaken herself to the hill. (Refrain.) 2. And carried with her thy skin-bag of meal. 3. And the wooden dish in which was thy butter. 4. May that day never come on which she will return !

Maolruainidh-Ghlinneachain was a silly, wandering woman, who forsook her child, when a good fairy found it, and lulled it to sleep with the above song.—F. T.

This interesting form of overlapping verse, in which each new stanza retains the last line of the previous one (not counting the refrain), is found also amongst Scandinavian ballads and the songs of French sailors. Such a verse-form suggests improvisation in the growth of these songs, whether or not the form itself may arise, as seems possible, from a former custom of two or more persons improvising verses alternately, each singer taking up the last line of his rival or companion and adding to it a new one of his own, which in turn the other must repeat, and pair with a second line. The words as well as the pattern of this pretty little song of Maolruaini suggest that it might easily be extended at the fancy of the singer.

The tune (though in a gapped scale), together with " An téid thu bhuain mhaoraich " (No. 25), in which a sharp 6th occurs as a grace-note, and " Nuair theid thu dh' Airigh Bhuachain " (No. 104), most resemble Dorians of any tunes I have noticed in this collection, in which Dorian tunes are conspicuously rare.—A. G. G.

The verse-form referred to above is, of course, a very favourite one in French poetry ; it seems to be even more usual in Highland song. In Russia the form is very commonly found in folk-song ; for many examples of its use, by solo and chorus alternating, *see* Eugenie Lineff's *Peasant Songs of Great Russia*, St. Petersburg, 1905 (D. Nutt, Long Acre, London), 1st series.—L. E. B.

31.—NA TRÌ EÒIN.

(THE THREE BIRDS.)

SUNG BY MARY ROSS,
FROM KILLMALUAG, SKYE, 1906.

Mode 3. a. b [with ♭7th]. (7-note scale.)

Moderate.

Na   trì   Eò - in chruinn-e gheal - a, Chruinn - e gheal - a, chruinn - e gheal-a, Na

185

tri Eò - in chruinn-e gheal-a, Chòir a' Bhail - e, Shuidh-eadh 'àd. Na tri Eò - in

chruinn - e gheal - a dhonn, Chruinn - e gheal - a dhonn, chruinn - e gheal - a

Fine.

dhonn. Na tri Eò - in chruinn-e gheal - a dhonn, B 'e sud na tri Eòin.

TRANSLATION.

The three birds, plump and white, plump and white, plump and white, the three birds, plump and white, were sitting near our home. The three birds, plump, white and brown (*repeat as before*). These were the three birds (*or*, the three wonderful birds !).

A full version of the words appears in the *Macdonald Coll.* (1911), p. 337.—F. T.

32.—COLANN GUN CHEANN.

(THE HEADLESS BODY.)

SUNG BY MRS. MACPHERSON (MARY MACDONALD),
POETESS, AT CONTIN MANSE, ROSS-SHIRE, 1870.

Mode 4. *b.* (6-note scale.)

Moderate.

'S fhad - a bhuam fhéin, bonn Beinn Ead - orr - a ; 'S fhad - a bhuam fhéin

Beal - ach a Mhòr - bheinn ; 'S fhad-a bhuam fhéin bonn Beinn Ead - orr - a

'S fhad - a gun teag-amh bhuam Beal - ach a Mhòr - bheinn O bhonn, gu bonn,

bonn Beinn Ead-orr', O Bhonn gu bonn, Beal-ach a Mhòr-bheinn. O bhonn gu bonn,

Fine.

bonn Beinn Ead - orr - a, 'S fhad-a gun teag - amh bhuam Beal-ach a Mhòr - bheinn.

186

Far from me is the base of Ben-Edar, and far from me is the pass of Morven, etc. From base to base, the base of Ben-Edar, from base to base, the pass of Morven, etc.

Colann-gun-Cheann belonged originally to the district of Trotternish in Skye, whence, being a malignant being who hated mankind, he was banished for his wicked practices, and, after wandering about, took up his abode near Arisaig on the mainland. He had not long been there, when the inhabitants, discovering his evil character, condemned him to death, and cut off his head. But he nevertheless continued to be a cause of danger and consternation in that locality, for he was in the habit of amusing himself by floating in the air at a certain narrow pass, throwing his head down on people going that way, and killing them. A young man of courage went forth to have an encounter with him, and on reaching the pass caught the descending head on the point of a sword and refused to give it back to Colann (the body,) till he promised to return to his own country-side. It was then he sang the above lament in consideration of the distance there was to traverse ere he could reach Ben-Edar, and the pass of Morven, near Quiraing, in Trotternish. After that, he was never again seen near Arisaig.—F. T.*

In J. F. Campbell's MS. collection, vol. xvii. p. 212, there is a twenty-two line fragment of a ballad under the same title, in which a "body without a head replaces the hideous, dirty and unkempt draggletail [of other versions] who begs shelter of the Feinn successively, and obtains her boon only from Diarmid." "The Daughter of King Under-waves" (Campbell's *Pop. Tales*, No. 86, iii. 403 f.) is another form of the same story, paralleled by an episode in the Norse saga of Hrólfr Kraki; and "The Marriage of Sir Gawain" and "King Henry" are English ballads on the same theme.—A. G. G.

33.—'NUAIR THIG MO BHODACH-SA DHACHAIDH.

(WHEN MY OLD MAN COMES HOME.)

Mode 4. *a.* (6-note scale.) SUNG BY MARY ROSS,
Moderate. FROM KILLMALUAG, SKYE, AT OBAN, 1898.

1. 'Nuair thig mo Bhod - ach - sa dhach-aidh, Hi - rì, ri - rì, ri-ri 'm bò - hò!

* See *Appendix* for further notes on this song.

187

Cha'n ann orm-sa ni è farr-aid. O - ho hao - ri, h-o'm bò.

2. *Cha'n ann orm-sa ni è farraid
   Hi-ri-ri-ri, ri-ri 'm bò-hò.
   Ach air a' bharr bhiodh air a' bhainne.
   O-ho hao-ri, ho'm bò.

3. No air an ubh bhiodh anns a' chliabh.

4. No air a' mhin bhiodh anns a' bhalg.

5. 'S truagh nach robh Bodaich an Domhain.

6. Air muir lom, no'n caolas domhain.

7. 'S mo Bhodach-sa 'n an teis-meadhon.

* In this song the second line of each verse becomes the first of the succeeding couplet.—F. T.

TRANSLATION.

1. When my old man comes home, (hi-ri, etc.) it is not for me that he enquires, (O-hó, etc.) 2. It is not for me that he enquires, (hi-ri, etc.) but about the cream that has come on the milk, (O-hó, etc.) 3. or the egg that may be in the creel, 4. or the amount of meal in the bag. 5. Oh, pity that all the old men in the world were not 6. on the open sea, or on a deep sound, 7. and my old fellow in their midst !

34.—CIOD È 'GHAOIL ?

(WHAT IS IT, LOVE?)

SUNG BY MISS ISABEL CAMERON, FROM THE ISLAND OF
MULL, WHO LEARNED IT FROM HER NURSE, A NATIVE
OF THE ISLAND OF EIGG.

Mode 2. *a.*
Slow.

1. "''Dé a Ghaoil a bhith-eadh ort?" "O cha'n fhios-am, Ach cha'n ith mi mìr an nochd!"

2. "An è do cheann a bhith goirt?" (Refrain).

3. "An è do mhàthair a ghabh ort" (Refrain).

TRANSLATION.

1. *Verse:* "What ails thee, my love?" *Refrain:* "Oh, I know not ! But I will not eat a morsel to-night." 2. *Verse:* "Does thy head ache?" *Refrain:* "Oh, I," etc. 3. *Verse:* Is it thy mother has punished thee?" *Refrain:* "Oh, I," etc.

The close correspondence of the melody to the words, and the strangely symmetrical form of the former, make this a very remarkable song, perhaps a fragment of some longer ballad of the "Lord Randal" type.—J. A. F. M.

The subject of the "Lord Randal" class of ballad is a favourite one in Scandinavian countries, and well may have been brought from thence to the Hebrides. I have a Ross-shire version (with English words), sung by a Gaelic-speaking person. The above tune, like "Caoidh Leannain," No. 101 in this collection, has a striking likeness to some Russian folk-songs.—L. E. B.

This song was noted by Mrs. Kennedy Fraser from Miss Tolmie's singing, and appears in a slightly different form in *Songs of the Hebrides*, as "A Soothing Croon from Eigg." The melody is formed on four notes only.—A. G. G.

35.—GAOL NAM BAN.

(MOST LOVED OF WOMEN.)

Mode 4. *b.* (6-note scale.)

Slow.

SUNG BY MARY ROSS, FROM KILLMALUAG, SKYE, 1907.

(Man.)

1. "Gaol nam ban thu, Gràdh nam ban thu! Cò aig a dh'fhàg thu na caor-aich?

(Wife.)

Gaol nam ban thu, Gràdh nam ban thu!" "Ag - ad fhéin gu dean - amh aod - aich."

(Man.)

"'Si sin a chòir! 'Si sin a chòir! 'Si sin a chòir! Och-òin a Righ!

Fine.

Cùm o'n Loch mi, 'S na leig 'gam bhàth - adh mi!"

2. "Cò aig a dh'fhàg thu na gobhair?"
   "Agad fhéin gu n dean thu 'm bleoghain."

TRANSLATION.

1. (*Husband*) "Thou dearest, and most loved among women! To whom hast thou left the sheep? Thou dearest, etc." (*Dying wife*) "To thyself, for making raiment." (*Husband*) "That is justice. (*or* my due) [*thrice*]. Ochoin, O Lord, do Thou keep me from the loch, and do not let me drown myself!" 2. (*Husband*) "To whom hast thou left the goats?" (*Wife*) "To thee, that thou mayest milk them." (*Husband*) "That is justice," etc.

An old woman at Killmaluag, Skye, used to croon this song to herself, when sitting at her wheel spinning, or when out herding her cow, more than sixty years ago.—F. T.

36.—EÓGHANN BAN.

(EOGHAN THE FAIR-HAIRED.)

PENTATONIC.
Mode 3.

SUNG BY MRS. ARCH. MACDONALD,
CLEADALE, EIGG, 1902.

O - Hó! Luaidh nan gill-ean; Eir - ibh eil - e! Eógh-ainn Bhàin! O-hó! Ghaoil nan gill-ean! Eir - ibh eil - e! Eógh-ainn Bhàin! Ó - hó! Luaidh nan gill-ean! Eir-ibh eil - e! Eógh-ainn Bhàin. Cha 'n eil cron ri luaidh dhuit, Mur ith-eadh tu fuar - ag; Bun-tàt - a as a luath - ainn, Biodh e fuar no blàth.

TRANSLATION.

Refrain: O dearest of boys! (Eiribh eile!) Eoghan the fair-haired! (O-hó!) Beloved of boys, (Eiribh eile!) Eoghan the fair-haired! *Verse*: No harm is there to tell of thee unless thou didst eat "crowdie,"* or potatoes from the ashes, either hot or cold. (R.)

The above words and tune used to be sung to Eoghan Bàn by his nurse, in the island of Eigg, about the year 1769.—F. T.

37.—THA CHU'AG IS "GUG-GÙG" AICE.

(THE CUCKOO CALLS.)

PENTATONIC.
Mode 2.

SUNG BY JESSIE MACDOUGALL, SERVANT AT NAIRN,
FROM MOIDART, INVERNESS-SHIRE, 1870.

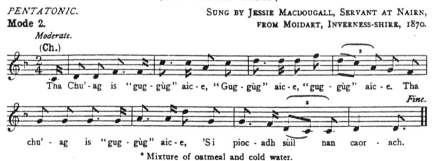

Tha Chu'- ag is "gug - gùg" aic - e, "Gug - gùg" aic - e, "gug - gùg" aic - e. Tha chu'- ag is "gug - gùg" aic - e, 'S i pioc - adh sùil nan caor - ach.

* Mixture of oatmeal and cold water.

190

1. Chunna mi, s gu'm b'fhiosrach mi,
   Na ròin a falbh le litrichean,
   Màileid is pailios orra,
   Is iad cho glic ri daoine.

   (Ch.)

2. Chunna mi na partanan
   A danns' air ùrlar charbadan
   A chorra-ghritheach is bat aice,
   'S i 'cur a steach nan caorach.

   (Ch.)

3. Fhuair mi nead an tàrmachain
   Ann talamh-toll 's an àrd-dhorus ;

An dreathan-donn 's dà ràmh aige
'Cur bàt' an aghaidh gaoithe.

   (Ch.)

4. Chunna mi na cudaigean
   A sniomh air an cuid chuigealan,
   An iolair(e) mhór is buideal aic
   A falbh an cuideachd dhaoine.

   (Ch.)

5. Chunna mi na donnagan
   Is cuailtean móra chonnaidh orr' ;
   An fhaochag bheag 's an donnalaich
   A falbh le dronnaig fhraoich oirr'.

   (Ch.)

TRANSLATION.

(*Chorus*: The cuckoo is calling cuckoo ! cuckoo ! while picking out the eyes of the sheep.) 1. I beheld, being well-informed, the seals going about delivering letters, dressed in a pelisse with a wallet, and looking as wise as men. 2. I have seen crabs on the floor of chariots, and the heron with a staff driving home the sheep. 3. I saw the ptarmigan in an earth-hole in the door-lintel, and the wren with a pair of oars pulling a boat against the wind. 4. And I saw young "saithe" * spinning off their distaffs, and the grand eagle carrying a cask in the company of men. 5. Cockles I have seen bearing heavy loads of fuel, and the little whelk howling under a burden of heather.

It is said that this song was composed in one night by a young woman who was promised the life of her brother, a prisoner under sentence of death, if she could sing in the morning a song in which there must not be one word of truth. Having by this production fulfilled the necessary conditions, her petition was granted, and, with her brother restored to her, she went home rejoicing.—F. T.

For similar nonsense-songs—perhaps originally founded on the same story—*see* "The Man to the Green Joe" (Christie's *Traditional Airs*, vol. ii. p. 192, also in Buchan's collection) and "Neerie, Norrie" (Ford's *Vagabond Songs of Scotland*), a song which is candidly admitted to be "A' big lees frae the head to the tail." There is a similar song in Welsh called "The Seven Wonders" ("Y Saith Rhyfeddod") printed in Part 3 of the *Welsh Folk-Song Journal.*—A. G. G.

This nonsense-song seems to be closely allied to the farcical animal-songs beloved by the French peasantry. For good examples, *see* "Chansons Boufonnes" in Soleville's *Chants Populaires du Bas-Quercy* (1889); Montel and Lambert's *Chants Populaires du Languedoc* (p. 515), and Champfleury and Weckerlin's *Chansons Populaires des Provinces de France*, p. xviii. Fantastic animal-behaviour does not seem a favourite subject in English folk-song, though examples (such as "There was a pig went out to dig," and "The Derby Ram" in *English County Songs*) are not wanting.—L. E. B.

* Young coal-fish.

VOCAL DANCE MUSIC ("PUIRT-A-BEUL").

38.—DHOMHNUILL, A DHOMHNUILL!

(DONALD, O DONALD.)

Mode 2. *a.* (6-note scale.)

Sung in the Nursery at Bracadale Manse, Skye, 1861.

Lively.

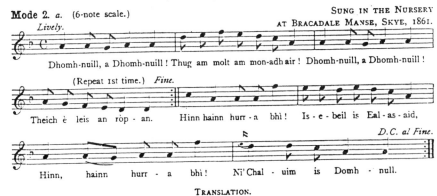

Dhomh-nuill, a Dhomh-nuill! Thug am molt am mon-adh air! Dhomh-nuill, a Dhomh-nuill!

(Repeat 1st time.) *Fine.*

Theich è leis an ròp - an.   Hinn hainn hurr - a   bhì!   Is - e - beil is Eal - as - aid,

D.C. al Fine.

Hinn,   hainn   hurr - a   bhì!   Ni' Chal - uim   is   Domh - null.

TRANSLATION.

Donald, O Donald, the wether is away to the moor; with the tether he is gone! Hinn, etc., etc. Isabella and Elizabeth, Calum's girl, and Donald!

Similar puerile verses are attached to the dance-tunes of some other nations. *E.g.* there is a Norwegian dance, the music of which goes to these absurd words:

> "My billy-goat, my billy-goat bites the bark of the trees.
> I think he is mad! I think he is mad!"

The above reel-tune is unlike the generality of Scottish reel-melodies, and strikes me as Scandinavian in character. *See* note to "Poca sìl an t-sealgair," No. 40 in this collection.—A. G. G.

39.—BROCHAN LOM, TANA LOM.

(GRUEL THIN AND MEAGRE.)

PENTATONIC (first 12 bars).

Mode 3. *b.*

Sung in the Nursery at Bracadale Manse, Skye, 1861.

Lively. Reel time.

(S.) V.

1. Broch-an lom,   tan - a lom ; Broch-an lom   sùgh - ain ; Broch-an lom,   tan - a lom,

S. R.

Broch-an tan - a sùgh - ain. Broch-an tan - a, tan - a, tan - a; Broch-an tan - a sùgh - ain;

Broch-an tan - a, tan - a, tan - a; Broch-an tan - a sùgh - ain; Broch-an tan - a, tan-a, tan - a,

Fine.

Broch-an tan - a sùgh - ain; Broch-an lom, tan - a lom. Broch-an tan - a sùgh - ain.

(S.)V.

2. Thug-aibh ar - an dha*na gill-ean, Leis a bhroch-an shùgh-ain. Thug-aibh ar - an dha na gill-ean;

Leis a bhroch-an shùgh-ain; Thug-aibh ar - an dha na gill-ean, Leis a bhroch-an shùgh-ain,

R.

D.C. dal Segno al Fine.

Broch - an lom, tan - a lom, Broch - an tan - a sùgh - ain.

* *dialect* = do.

3. Sud an rud a gheibheamaid 'o nighean gobh' an Dùine [*thrice*] (R. and *D.C.* R.).

TRANSLATION (without repetitions).

1. Gruel thin and meagre, gruel thin from sowans. 2. Give ye bread to the young men with the sowans-gruel. 3. This is what we used to get from the smith's daughter at the Dùn.

The above was a jocular song that arose about some ill-made porridge, which being very thin was declared to be like gruel, or even "sowans" (the fermented juice of oatmeal husks boiled, in bygone times a favourite article of food in Scotland).—F. T.

There is also a Gaelic nursery-song about "Brochan buirn" (water-gruel or porridge), the tune of which has been used for other songs, *e.g.* "Cruachan Beann." It is quite different from this reel-melody, of which a curious transformation may be seen in the tune attached to Lady Nairne's song "The Auld Hoose."—A. G. G.

Cf. another tune to similar words in *Puirt-a-beul.*—L. E. B.

193

40.—POCA SÌL AN T-SEALGAIR.

(THE HUNTSMAN'S BAG OF GRAIN.)

Mode 3. *a. b.* [with ♭7th].

Strathspey time.

SUNG IN THE NURSERY
AT BRACADALE MANSE, SKYE, 1861.

2. *Chunnacas a tighinn è,
   Cha 'n fhacas a falbh è.

3. B'fhoghainteach i, beadarrach i,
   B'aigeannach an t-seana bhean.

* Each couplet is sung thrice, ending with a line of refrain.

TRANSLATION.

1. *Ref. and Verse*: Among ye, the huntsman's bag of grain. The bag which he was carrying, the burden that was on him, as he was going along. 2. It was seen coming, but was not seen going! 3. Active, playful, and spirited was the old woman!

This version of mine appears in *Puirt-a-beul,* p. 12. The song was sung by two persons or sets of singers who took lines alternately and beat time with their hands. The words "sealgair" and "falbh" were sung with the extra vowel as written under the music.—F. T.

This is a very interesting dance-rhythm and quite different from the usual type of reel and strathspey tunes, the former of which, especially, are generally extremely unvocal in character. It seems possible that Norse influence is traceable in some of these *port-a-beul* tunes (*cf.* "Dhomhnuill a Dhomhnuill" and "Brochan Lom," Nos. 38 and 39). There is a Danish "Goosegirl's Song" in *Børnenes Musik* very similar in character to "Poca sil an t-sealgair," and with a like insistent refrain, imitating the cackle of geese. The scattering of the bag of grain suggests a possible connection between the two songs—both apparently dance measures.

The intrusion of an extra syllable into *falbh* and *sealgair*—sung *fal-abh* and *seal-a-gair*—illustrates a well-marked characteristic not only of English folk-song but also of Hessian and Swiss, and probably other European folk-music as well—an eccentricity of pronunciation arising simply from the presence of an extra note in the music, which note, instead of being slurred over (the plan which would be adopted by a cultured singer), is given its proper accent by being accommodated with an extra syllable. So in English folk-song we have "sweet-a-ly" for "sweetly" or "wor-dle-king" for "walking," and find a similar interpolated "o" or "a" in the middle of a Swiss or German word, when required by the exigencies of the tune.—A. G. G. [Yet often in spoken Gaelic these so-called 'parasitic' vowels arise quite naturally in certain combinations of consonants.—G. H.]

GAASEPIGENS SANG.

(GOOSEGIRL'S SONG.)

From *Børnenes Musik.*

Gæk, gæk, gæk, gæk, gæk, gæk, gæk.

Gæk, gæk, gæk, gæk, gæk.

Gæk, gæk, gæk, gæk, gæk, gæk, gæk.

Gæk, gæk, gæk, gæk, gæk.

GROUP II.—SONGS OF LABOUR.

WAULKING SONGS.

SLOW TYPE.

41.—GRIOGAL CRIDHE.

(BELOVED GREGOR.)

Mode 3. *a.* [with ♭7th] (6-note scale.)
MIXOLYDIAN INFLUENCE.

A MEMORY FROM EARLIEST DAYS
IN DUIRINISH AND MINGINISH, SKYE, 1908.—F. T.

Slow. (S.)

1. 'S iom - a h-oidh - che fhliuch is thior - am, Sìd - e na seachd si-an,

Gheibh - eadh Griog - al dhomh - sa creag - an, Ris an gabh - ainn di-on.

(Ch.)

Òbh - an! Òbh - an! Òbh - an - i - ri! Òbh - an - i - ri ò

Òbh - an! Òbh - an! Òbh - an - i - ri! 'S mór mo mhul-ad 's mór.

Fine.

2. Dhìrich mi dh'an t-seòmar mhullaich,
'S theirinn mi 'n tigh-làir,
'S cha d 'fhuair mise Griogal cridhe
'Na shuidhe mu 'n chlàr.
(Ch.)

3. Eudail mhóir, a shluagh an Domhain,
Dhòirt iad t' fhuil o 'n dé,
'S chuir iad do cheann air stob daraich
Tacan beag bho d' chré.
(Ch.)

4. B 'annsa bhi le Griogal cridhe
Teàrnadh chruidh le gleann,

Na le Baran mór na Dalach,
Sìoda geal mu m' cheann.
(Ch.)

5. Cha n 'eil ùbhlan idir agam,
'S ùbhlan uil' aig càch,
'S ann tha m'ùbhlan-s' cùbhr' ri caineal
'S cùl an cinn ri làr.
(Ch.)

6. 'Nuair a bhios mnàthan òg a' bhaile,
'Nochd nan cadal sèimh,
'S ann bhios mis' air bruaich do lice,
'Bualadh mo dhà làimh.
(Ch.)

196

1. Many a night of rain, or fair, or tempest raging wild, Gregor would find for me a rock, and shelter from the storm. (*Cho.* : Obhan, etc. Great is my grief, and great!) 2. I climbed to the room above and searched the room below, but did not find Gregor, beloved, sitting at the board. 3. Most loved of all men in the world, they shed thy blood since yesterday ; on oaken stake they set thy head, near where thy body lay. 4. Far rather would I be with Gregor, herding down the glen, than with the great Baron of Dull, and white silk round my head. 5. No apples now be mine, such as the others have, yet fragrant are mine as cinnamon, their heads low on the ground. 6. When other women lie to-night, in peaceful slumber still, beside thy grave there shall I lie, smiting my two hands.

The above lullaby is well known throughout the Hebrides, though the incidents mentioned in it occurred on the mainland. The subject is the mourning of a young lady, a daughter of Campbell of Glenlyon, for the death of her husband, Grigor Roy, an outlawed MacGregor, who was executed at Kenmore, on Loch Tay, by command of Sir Colin Campbell of Glenurchy, in 1570. See *Celtic Review*, App. 15, 1909. In *Lyra Celtica* (p. 191) there is a metrical translation into English of this song. There is also a version in Gaelic, with a melody, in *Binneas nam Bard* (Bardic Melody), p. 48. My Gaelic verses and air have already appeared in the *Gesto Coll.* (App. p. 25). *Cf.* the air with that of "Cumha Dhiarmad," No. 88 in this collection. A version is also given in the Rev. Maclean Sinclair's *Gaelic Bards*, published in Cape Breton, Nova Scotia, and yet another text in the *Macdonald Collection* (1911).—F. T.

42.—ORAN MU'N GHRUAGAICH.

(A SONG ABOUT THE GRUAGACH.)

PENTATONIC.
Mode 3.

SUNG BY OIGHRIG * [EFFIE] ROSS (COTTAR),
BRACADALE, SKYE, 1861.

1. Chaor - ain nach deàn thu sol - us dhomh ! E-hò hi ri, rith ibh ò hó. Gus am faic mi fear àrd a bhroill - ich ghil ! E-hò hì ri, rith ibh ò hò, Hi rì, hò - rionn ò.

* Affraic, (name of an abbess of Kildare,) Aithbric, Effric, a nymph name as in Glen Affric? The root seemingly *breac* = spotted (the prefix '*ath*' again signifying 'repetition ').—G. H.

2. *Buachaille luaineach mu bhruachan a'ghlinne-s' thu,
   Air an d'fhàs a'ghruag 'na clannaibh air!

3. 'S mis a' bhean bhochd tha gu brònach
   'S mi 's a' ghleannan so 'nam ònar (aonar).

4. 'S mis a' bhean bhochd tha gu cràidhteach,
   'S mi 'gad chàradh, laoigh do mhàthar.

5. 'S mi gun phiuthar! 'S mi gun bhràthair.
   Rìgh nan dùl! bi teachd làimh rium.

* The first line of every verse is followed by the solo refrain, and the second line by the chorus; and the last line of each verse forms the first line of the next.

TRANSLATION.

O ember, do thou give me light, (*Refrain*: Ehò, etc.) so that I may behold him who is of lofty stature, and white bosom; (*Ch.*: Ehò, etc.), 2. swift-footed herdsman on the slopes of the glen, on whose head the hair has grown in curling locks! 3. Oh, a sorrowful woman am I, mourning solitary in this glen; 4. sorely afflicted, and in anguish, laying thee out, thou darling of thy mother. 5. Having no sister nor a brother, King of Nature, be thou near me!

The subject of this song is the lamentation of a mother over her daughter, who had died in a strange manner when they were staying together at a sheiling in a lonely part of Glen-Macaskill. One evening when gathering the cows into the fold, a cow becoming restive, the young woman drove her in with rude words and blows. But the Friend of the Cattle, known as the Gruagach, (occasionally assuming the appearance of a beautiful youth with long golden hair and a wonderfully white bosom,) was at that moment, though invisible, standing near, and on his smiting the girl with a rod which he always had in his hand, she straightway fell down dead. Her mother was mourning over her all night, and the Gruagach, leaning against the upper beam of the dwelling, gazed at her till break of day, when he vanished. The above tune, with Gaelic words, has been contributed by me to the *Gesto Coll.* (App. p. 19).—F. T.

43.—CUMHA MHIC-LEÒID.

(LAMENT FOR MACLEOD.)

Mode 5. *a. b.* (7-note scale.)   SUNG BY RODERICK MACLEOD (COTTAR),
PHRYGIAN INFLUENCE.   BRACADALE, SKYE, 1862.

Slow.

1. Mo   shàth   ghal   goirt,   Mar a   ta   mi   an nochd! 'S mi gun

tàmh, gun f hois, gun sunnd! Mo shàth ghal goirt, Mar a

Fine.

ta mi an nochd! 'S mi gun tàmh, gun f hois, gun sunnd!

2. 'S mi gun sunnd air stà ;
   Gun mo dhùil ri bhi slàn ;
   Tha mo shùgradh gu bràth air chùl.
   (Repeat as chorus.)

3. 'S ann tha Leòdach mo ghaoil,
   'S an oll-anart chaol,
   'S gun chòmhdach ri thaobh, ach bùird.
   (Ch.)

4. 'Sè bhi smaointinn ort,
   So-chràidh mi'm chorp,
   'Sa chnàmh na ruisg bho m'shùil.
   (Ch.)

[Màiri Nigh'n Alasdair Ruaidh,
17th century.]

TRANSLATION.

1. In the state in which I am this night, I am satiated with sore weeping ; without rest, without peace or joy. 2. With health uncertain, and of recovery there being no hope, my gladness is for ever gone. 3. For Macleod, beloved, is in a fine woollen shroud, with no covering to his side but boards. 4. It is with thinking on thee that my body has been in acute suffering, and the lashes worn away from my eyes.   [By Mary Macleod, 17th century.]

This was sung by the bardess at the bedside of her chief, Macleod of Dunvegan, when he pretended that he had died. Each verse is sung twice. My version of the air, with Gaelic words, is included in the *Gesto Coll.* (App. p. 53).—F. T.

Cf. the tune with that of "Caoidh Màthar," No. 49 in this collection. Mode 5 (of my schedule) is one which lends itself to peculiar pathos, particularly when its first gap becomes filled by the minor 2nd, in which case it assumes the character of the Phrygian Mode and deepens in its capacity for expressing a tender and brooding melancholy. Other Scottish tunes founded upon this mode are "The Bridegroom grat" (the original tune to which "Auld Robin Gray" was written) ; "Drowned," an old Highland melody from the Arisaig district included in *Songs of the North*; and in this collection "Hóró lail Ó" (No. 54), "Ba-bà a leinibh" (No. 3), "Iuraibh o-hì" (No. 75), etc. There are several psalm-tunes in the Phrygian Mode in the *Scottish Psalter* of 1635, and Mendelssohn has made beautiful use of it in "Elijah" to the words "Lord, bow thine ear to our prayer," where it well conveys a feeling of almost hopeless sorrow and yearning to the listener's mind. This mode is very rare in English folk-song, and apparently unknown in Irish folk-music.—A. G. G.

199

44.—CHALL Ò RO HÌ.

Mode 2. *a. b.* (7-note scale.)
AEOLIAN INFLUENCE.
Slow.

Sung by Oighrig Ross (Cottar),
Bracadale, Skye, 1861.

(a) Chall ò rò hì, è hò i. Na hi rì, ri ibh ò hi, iur-aibh ò.

(b) 1. Tha bric air Linn - e na h-iùbh-raich. (c) Chall ò ribh ò hò. i - ùr - aibh ò.

2. Tha féidh air Leacainn-a-smùdain.
3. A rì, ma ta! Ciod è sin dùinne.
4. Cha bheò Ailean, 's cha mhaireann Rùraidh.
5. Mo dheagh fhear-taigh 'na luigh 'san Dùnan.

6. Dh'eirich mi gu moch 'sa mhaduinn.
7. Is shuidh mi air Cnocan-an-fhasgaidh ;
8. A rì, ma rinn ! Gu 'n do leig mi osnaich.

The above lines take the position of (b) in each round.

TRANSLATION.

(*Chorus*: Chall ò, etc.) 1. There are salmon in the pool of the grove-of-yew-trees, (*Refrain*: Chall ò, etc., followed by Chorus) 2. and deer on the slope-of-the-rolling-mist. 3. Alas, what matter to us? 4. Alan is not living, and Rury is no more, 5. and my excellent husband lying in the tower. 6. I rose early in the morning, 7. and was sitting on the knoll-of-shelter. 8. Alas! and if I were, then gave I forth sighs !

45.—LÀ MILLEGÀRAIDH.

(THE DAY* OF MILLEGÀRAIDH.)

Mode 3. *a* [with ♭7th]. (6-note scale.)
Slow.

Sung by Oighrig Ross (Cottar),
Bracadale, Skye, 1861.

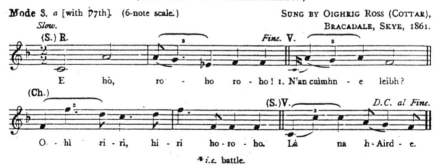

E hò, ro - ho ro - ho ! 1. N'an cuìmhn - e leibh ?

O hì rì - rì, hi - rì ho - ro - ho. Là na h-Aird - e.

* *i.e.* battle.

200

2. *Na 'n là eile,
   Millegàraidh?

3. Bha fir an sin
   Air dhroch càradh,

4. An druim fòdh',
   'S am buinn bhàn ris.

5. N'an cuimhne leibh,
   Là Allt Eirinn,

6. Na 'n là eile,
   Uamh-deirge?

7. Chunnacas bàta
   Falbh gu siùbhlach;

8. 'S i dol tiomchioll,
   Rudha h-Ùinis;

9. As a sin gu
   Rudh'-an-Dùnain.

10. B'è mo leannan
    Bha 'ga stiùireadh,

11. Beul 'ga éubhadh,
    Làmh 'ga h-iomradh;

12. 'S ioma bean bhochd
    Bha gu cràidhteach,

13. 'S i gun mhac ann,
    'S i gun bhràthair,

14. Gun duin' ann a
    Ghabhadh bàigh dhi.

15. 'S mo mhollachd sin
    Aig Clann-Rànuill!

* Interpolate the S. and Ch. refrains throughout. as in the first verse, ending with the S. refrain.

TRANSLATION.

(*Refrain*: E-hò, etc.) 1. Remember ye (*Ch.*: O-hi, etc.) the day of the Aird, (R.) 2. or that other of Millegàraidh? 3. Men were there in sad condition, 4. lying prone, showing the white soles of their feet. 5. Remember ye the day of Auldearn, 6. or that other of Uamh-deirge? 7. A boat was seen going swiftly, 8. turning round Rudha-h-Unais, 9. and from there to Rudh-an-Dunain. 10. It was my lover who was steering; 11. mouth calling, hand rowing. 12. Many a woman was sorely grieving, 13. missing her son there, having no brother, 14. and no man left to delight in her. 15. May my malediction be with Clan-Ranald!

There were dreadful feuds and forays between the Macleods of Skye and Harris and the Macdonalds of Clan-Ranald in the days of old. The battle at Millegaraidh in Waternish, 1570, has been kept in remembrance as the last occasion on which the fairy flag of Dunvegan was unfurled, and with disastrous consequences to the invaders from the Clan-Ranald territories, who, falling under the spell of the flag, which made them see a vast concourse of armed men where there was in reality a much smaller gathering, fled in a panic to their galleys, and were almost all cut down ere they reached the shore.—F. T.

46.—CUMHA BHRAITHREAN.

(LAMENT FOR BROTHERS.)

Sung by Janet Anderson (Nurse), Manse of Contin, Ross-shire, 1870.

Mode 3. *a.* (6-note scale.)
Moderate.

Hù ò - rò, hù ò. Rò - hò ù - ò hì ò. Hù ò - rò, hù ò. 1. Gur h-è mis - e tha fo mhul - ad, Tha leann-dubh air mo ghruaidh.

2. *Cha b'è cumha mo leannain
Ged a dh'fhanadh è bhuam,

3. Ach a cumha mo bhràithrean
Tha cnàmh anns a' chuan.

4. Cumha Eachainn is Lachlainn
Dh'fhàg tana mo ghruag.

5. 'S oil leam diol'ur cùl clannach
'S an fheamainn 'ga luadh.

6. 'S tric mo shùil air an rudha,
Fodh'n bhruthaich ud shuas,

7. Ach am faic mi seòl bréid-gheal
Là gréine 'sa 'chuan.

8. Cha 'n 'eil long thig o 'n rudha,
Nach toir snidh air mo ghruaidh.

9. Cha 'n 'eil bàt thig 'sa' chaolas,
Nach caochail mo shnuadh.

10. Cha dhìrich mi bruthach,
'S cha shiubhail mi uair,

11. Cha dhean mi céum idir,
Gus an tig na bheil bhuam.

12. Cha chaidil mi còmhnard
A Dhòmhnach no Luain.

13. Tha bhur leabaidh na h-ònar,
Anns an t-seòmar ud shuas;

14. Cha teid mi 'ga càradh
Sibhs' a ghràidhean fad bhuam.

15. Gur h-è mis 'tha fo mhulad
Air an tulaich luim fhuair!

[Le 'm piuthar.] [By their sister.]

*The S. and Ch. refrains come before every verse, and after the last.

TRANSLATION.

(S.R. and Ch.) 1. Under what sorrow am I! and tears are on my cheek! 2. It is not because of mourning for my lover, though he were to stay away, 3. but lamenting for my brothers, who are lying dead in the sea. 4. Grieving for Hector and Lachlan has thinned my hair. 5. The state of your locks, being waulked in the sea-ware, distresses me sore! 6. My gaze is often towards the promontory below yonder hill-side, 7. in the hope that I may descry a white sail, on a day of sunshine, out at sea. 8. There is no ship coming round the headland that brings not tears upon my cheek; 9. and no boat appears in the Sound without causing my colour to change. 10. I cannot climb the slope, nor walk for an hour; 11. I cannot move a step, till they return whom I mourn. 12. In peace I am unable to sleep either on Sunday or Monday! 13. Your bed is forsaken in the chamber above, 14. and I cannot arrange it, while ye, beloved, are away. 15. Most mournful am I, on the bare, chilly knoll!

47.—ILL IÙ, HILL Ó, ILLEAN IS Ó.

Mode 3. *a. b.* [with ♭7th]. (7-note scale.)

Rather slow.

SUNG BY MARY ROSS,
FROM KILLMALUAG, SKYE, AT OBAN, 1898.

Ill iù, hill ó, ill - ean is ó. Hill iù ò, cha
d'fhuair mi 'n cad-al. Ill iù, hill ó, ill - ean is ó. 1. Cha d 'fhuair mi 'n cad - al
an raoir, 'S gur goirt na saighd - ean rinn mo ghlac - adh.

2. *Cha d 'fhuair mi'n cadal an raoir,
   Ag ionndrainn a choibhneis a chleachd mi.

3. 'S muladach, 's muladach a tha mi,
   'S mi'm aonar air Airigh-bhadain.

4. 'G iomain a chrodh-laoigh gu buaile,
   'S gun am buachaill' a bhith agam.

5. 'G iomain a chrodh-laoigh gu àirigh,
   Gun thu ghràidh a bhith 'n am fhaisge.

6. Mo ghaol do làmh gheal gun chll.
   An déidh a sìneadh anns an anart.

* The S. and Ch. refrains come before each verse and after the last.

TRANSLATION.

(*Refrain*: Ill iù, etc., *Chorus*: Hill, iù, etc.) 1. Last night I could not sleep, for distressing were the arrows which had reached me. (R. followed by Ch.) 2. I could not get any sleep last night, missing the kindness to which I had been accustomed. 3. Mournful, mournful, and solitary am I, on Airigh-bhadain, 4. herding the cattle to the fold, without, alas, the herdsman with me ; 5. driving the milk-cows to the sheiling, and thou, beloved, not at my side. 6. Dear to me is thy pale hand, lifeless and laid out in linen.

A very characteristic and expressive tune. The refrain seems to be a cattle-call, like a similar one attached to the song "Hill-ean is ó hùg ù" ("The cattle are lowing in the pasture"), No. 66 in this collection.—A. G. G.

This air, of which I have a phonographed variant to other Gaelic words, is unlike the generality of Scottish Highland tunes. Its descending opening phrase is of a kind very commonly found in Irish airs (*see* the complete *Petrie Collection*, Nos. 807 and 975); and it may originally have been one of those six-eight time melodies used indifferently in Ireland as a march or jig. The *Petrie Collection* gives many examples of these.—L. E. B.

48.—HÓ RIONN EILE.

Mode 1. *a.* [with ♭3rd]. (6-note scale.)

SUNG BY MARY ROSS,
FROM KILLMALUAG, SKYE, AT OBAN; 1899.

Slow.

"Hó rionn éil - e, O - hì a - hó! O - hì, ibh o, Hó - ró hù - ò.
Hó rionn éil - e, O - hì a - hò! 1. Ail - ein duinn beul a' mhànr-ain.

2. *Beul an t-sùgraidh, 'sa chiùil ghàire.
3. Righ nam fear! bu mhór mo ghràdh dhuit.
4. Gu 'n aithnichinn siubhal do bhàta
5. 'S tu fhéin a ghaoil air ràmh bràghad.
6. O gur mis 'tha air mo sgaradh
7. Gu bheil do leabaidh anns an fheamainn ;
8. Gur h-iad na ròin do luchd-faire

9. Do choinnlean àrd na reultan geala ;
10. 'S do cheòl-fìdhle gaoir na mara.
11. Fhaoileag bheaga, fhaoileag bhàn thu !
12. Thig a nall, is inn's do naigheachd.
13. C'àit an d'fhàg thu na fir gheala ?"
14. "Dh'fhàg mi iad 's an eilean mhara.
15. Cùl ri cùl, is iad gun anail."

*The refrains for solo and chorus come before every line and after the last one.

TRANSLATION.

(*Refrain:* Hó rìonn, etc., *Chorus:* Ohì, etc.) 1. "O Alan of the brown hair, mouth of tender tones, (R. followed by Ch.) 2. of mirth, and of melodious laughter! 3. Noblest among men, great was my devotion to thee. 4. I could recognise the movement of thy boat, 5. and thou, beloved, at the stroke-oar. 6. How it grieves me 7. that thy bed is the sea-ware; 8. that those who wake thee are the seals; 9. thy tall candles the shining stars; 10. and thy violin music the murmur of the sea. 11. O little gull, O white gull! 12. Come hither, and give me thy tidings. 13. Where hast thou left the dear [*lit.* white] men?" 14. "I left them on an island of the sea, 15. back to back, and without breath."

This tune would be pentatonic were it not for the ♭3rd linking the verse to the refrain.—A. G. G.

Cf. verses 7 and 8 with two in "Coisich a rùin," No. 53 in this collection.—L. E. B.

49.—CAOIDH MÀTHAR.
(A MOTHER'S MOURNING.)

Mode 5. *a.* (6-note scale.)

SUNG BY MARY ROSS,
FROM KILLMALUAG, SKYE, AT OBAN, 1896.

Slow.

Hi ri rì, ri rì, rith-ibh o - hò. Ho-rionn o - hì - ó, ò - ho eil - e. Hi-ri

204

rì,   rì rì, rith-ibh ò hò.   1. Mhàir - i bhàin   a bhroill - ich ghlé - ghil !

2. *Cha dhùisg glaodhaich thu no éigheach.   7. Cha fhreagair ; mo thruaighe mise !
3. Cha dhùisg an fhidheal 'ga gleúsadh,   8. Bha mi 'n raoir aig bruaich do lice.
4. No piob-mhór nam feadan éibhinn ;   9. Ma bha, cha b'fheairrde mo mhisneach,
5. Cha dhùisg glaodh do mhàthar fhéin thu.   10. 'S gu 'm b'fhurasd falbh gun fhios duit.
6. Mhàiri, nach freagair thu idir ?

* The refrains for solo and chorus come before every line and after the last one.

TRANSLATION.

(*Refrain* : Hi ri, etc., *Chorus* : Ho rionn, etc.) 1. Fair-haired Mary of the pure white bosom ! (R. followed by Ch.) 2. no cries will awaken thee, nor calling aloud. 3. The violin when being tuned may not rouse thee, 4. nor the bag-pipe with joyous chanter. 5. The wail of thy own mother cannot wake thee. 6. Mary, wilt thou not indeed reply? 7. Woe's me !—thou wilt not answer me. 8. Last night I was sitting beside thy grave ; 9. but no consolation did I receive there, 10. for it was too easy to come away unknown to thee.

I have noted a close variant of this air from the singing of Dr. Farquhar MacRae, a native of West Ross-shire, who learned it from Mr. Donald Paterson of Kintail, Ross-shire. Dr. MacRae uses it for "the Kintail Dirge" ("Chaidh Donnachadh 'na' bheinn "), a lament on one Duncan, killed by his stepfather.—L. E. B.

As regards the tune, *see* note to "Cumha Mhic-Leòid," No. 43.—A. G. G.

50.—BEAN MHIC A' MHAOIR† (i.).

(THE WIFE OF THE SON OF THE MAOR [OR BAILIFF].)

Mode 5. *a.*   (6-note scale.

Slow.   REMEMBERED FROM EARLY YOUTH
                          IN MINGINISH, SKYE, 1854.—F. T.

1. Cha b'è 'n ain - nis,   Hùg   Ó   Thug dh'an tràigh mi,   Hùg   Ó.

Cha b'è,   cha   b'è,   Hó   ri ri, ho ró.   Ach an t-àil-gheas. Hùg   Ó.

† From Latin *major*. "An officer of justice, a bailiff, a catchpole, messenger ; inferior officers of various capacities are so called." (See *Gaelic Dictionary*, Macleod and Dewar, 1839.)

50.—BEAN MHIC A' MHAOIR (ii.).

(THE WIFE OF THE SON OF THE MAOR [OR BAILIFF].)

Mode 1. *b.* (6-note scale.)

SUNG BY MRS. HECTOR MACKENZIE,
DUNVEGAN, SKYE, 1862.

Moderate.

(Ch.)

Eil - e chall - ain,　O ho　hi　rì.——— 1. Cha b'e 'n ain - nis!　O ho　hi　rì.———

2. *Cha b'è, cha b'è
   Ach an t-àilgheas.
   'S è 'n duileasg donn
   Rinn mo thàladh;

3. Thug gu sgeir mi
   Nach dean tràghadh.

4. 'S a nighean ud thall
   'N cois na tràghad,

5. Nach truagh leat fhéin
   Bean 'ga bàthadh!

6. Cha truagh, cha truagh!
   'S beag do chàs diom.

7. Sìn do chrios bhuat,
   Thoir do làmh dhomh,

8. No sgòd dhe d'bhreacain
   Ma 's è 's àill leat,

9. Feuch an dean mi
   Buille shnàmha.

10. Theirig dhachaidh,
    Innis tràth è!

11. Ceil e, ceil e
    Air mo mhàthair

12. Gus an éirich
    Grian am màireach.

13. Mo thruaigh an nochd
    Mo thriùir phàisdean!

14. Fear dhiubh bliadhna,
    Fear a dhà dhiubh.

15. 'S fear beag eile
    Dh'aois a thàladh.

16. Thig a churach [no bhirlinn]
    So am màireach.

17. Bithidh m'athair ann
    'S mo thriùir bhràithrean.

18. 'S bithidh Mac-a-Mhaoir ann
    Air ràmh-bràghad.

19. Fleasgach donn a'
    Mhìog-shuil tlàthmhoir,

20. Beul an t-sùgraidh,
    'S beul a' mhanrain;

21. 'S gheibh iad mis' an
    Déis mo bhàthadh.

22. Mo chòta gorm air
    Bharr an t-sàile;

23. 'S mo chuailean donn
    Air dhroch càradh;

24. Mo bhràisd airgid
    Air creig làimh rium;

25. 'S mo phaidirean
    'N lag mo bhràghad.

26. 'S buidhe dh'an té
    Théid 'nam àite.

27. Gheibh i modh ann,
    Ciall is nàire.

28. Gheibh i gobhair
    Bhios air àrd-bheann.

29. Gheibh i caoraich
    Mhaola, bhàna,

30. Is crodh-laoigh a'
    Ruith mu'n àirigh.

*The last two lines of each quatrain (as sung to the first tune) are repeated to form the first two of the next, with the refrain as before. For the second tune, the verse is one line.

1. It was not necessity · that took me to the shore · —No, no— · but desire.* 2. It was the brown dulse that allured me, 3. that led me to a rock from which there will be no ebb. 4. O maiden, yonder on the strand! 5. does it not grieve thee to see a woman drown? 6. No pity hast thou; little dost thou care! 7. Stretch out thy girdle to me, reach forth thine hand, 8. or a corner of thy plaid, if thou prefer, 9. that I may try to swim a stroke! 10. Hasten home, tell it early; 11. hide it, hide it from my mother 12. till the sun shall rise to-morrow! 13. Woe's me to-night, my three babes; 14. one a year old, one of them two years, 15. and another of the age to be rocked in a cradle. 16. Hither the skiff [or birlinn] will come to-morrow. 17. My father will be here, and my three brothers, 18. and the son of the Maor at the stroke-oar— 19. the handsome brown-haired young man, of tender-glancing, mirthful eyes, 20. of the caressing speech and song; 21. and me they shall find after that I shall have been drowned; 22. my blue skirt on the surface of the brine; 23. my brown coil of hair in disorder; 24. my silver brooch on a crag beside me; 25. my beads† in the hollow of my neck. 26. Fortunate shall it be for her who takes my place; 27. she shall meet with good sense there, with respect and modesty; 28. she shall have goats upon the high hills, 29. sheep hornless and white, 30. and calving-cows running around the sheiling.

I contributed this song with translation to the *Gesto Coll.*, but it appeared instead in *Puirt-a-beul*, p. 44. It was also known as "A' bhean eudach" (*i.e.* "The jealous Woman"). This was a well-known fulling-song and lullaby on the West Coast of Scotland, and sung to different tunes, of which two are given here. The office of Maor was one of great importance in the olden days,‡ and this Maor was a man of distinction and wealth. (The word is applied in a different sense in later times.) The wife of the son of the Maor was enticed to a rock at ebb-tide by a wicked, designing woman to gather dulse, and then, by some contrivance, left there to drown. The cruel woman was afterwards married to the husband of her whose death she thus caused, but proved unable to conceal her guilt, for he once overheard her repeating to herself her victim's words of entreaty and lamentation, and, filled with horror, put her away.—F. T.

51.—CUMHA SHEATHAIN.

(LAMENT FOR SHEHAN [SETHAN].)

PENTATONIC.
Mode 3.

SUNG BY MARY ROSS
FROM KILLMALUAG, SKYE, 1899.

Rather slow.
(S.) V.

1. 'S mairg thubh - airt rium - sa Gu'm bu bhean shubh - ach mi!

* The dots indicate the lines of the stanza, punctuated by the refrain.

† Rosary.   ‡ See Skene's *Celtic Scotland*, vol. iii. p. 54; Mor-maer.

dheur - ach, chumh-ach mi! Na hi ibh ò! O hao! O - ho!

*The last line of each couplet is the first of the next.

TRANSLATION.

1. *They were foolish who said to me that I was a joyful woman! (R.: Hì Rì, etc.) A woman in anguish, tearful, and lamenting am I. (Ch.) 2. A sister to Maiv [Mave, Mève], and to Brian of the yellow hair, and wife of great Shehan, the rover. 3. Were Shehan seen to rise early in a morn in May, many a heart would rejoice. 4. The darling of his foster-mother; the beloved of his spouse; and of his own mother the seven-fold love. 5. Shehan the proud; my glory, and the most dear! Now art thou in thy winter-house, without music, dancing and song. To-night is Shehan a dead man.

There will be a more complete version of the words of the above lament, in Gaelic and English, in a forthcoming volume of Dr. A. Carmichael's *Carmina Gadelica.*—F. T.

A version by Mrs. Mackellar, with translation, is given in the *Transactions of the Gaelic Society of Inverness* (vol. xiii.). The following I learnt and noted, from a company of singers, in a cottage at Dalibrog, South Uist, in 1892. It differs a good deal from Mrs. Mackellar's Lochaber variant. The poem is said to have been composed by a girl in memory of her drowned sweetheart. Stanzas 24 and 25 are apparently additions to the original song.

O hu ru o hi rìbh o hō
Nāo o ho ro o ho ho
O hū hū hō hū ro bhi o
Hū rū hirìbh i ō ho.

1. Is minic a chuala nach do dhinns e
   O hu ru o, etc.
   Gu 'n robh mo leannan am Minginish.
   O hū hū hō hū ro bhi o, etc.

2. Thuirt iad riumsa gu 'm b' 'bhean shubhach mi ;
   Bean bhochd chianail chràiteach dhubhach mi.

3. Is ioma àite rinn mi shiubhail leat
   Bha mi 'n Alba 's bha mi 'n Uist leat.

4. Bha mi 'n Eirinn Choigeimh Mu(mh)an leat
   S chlàist mi aifhrinn sa Choill Chumhai(n)g leat.

5. Bha mi 'n Cilledonan fo dhubhar leat
   Dh 'òl mi deòl* an tobar Chumhaig leat.

6. Bha mi 'n Ìle 's bha mi 'n Uist leat
   An Eriscai nan cùla dubha leat.

7. Is minic (= mairg) thuirt rium gu 'm b 'bhean shubhach mi
   Bean rosadach dheurach dhubhach mi.

*Sic

208

8. Na faighte Seadhan ri fhuasgladh
Thigeadh na bric o na bruachan.

9. Cha bhiodh bó dhubh no bó ghualfhionn
An iochdar no 'n uachdar na buaile.

10. Nach rachadh a ghaoil! ga d' fhuasgladh
'S bheireadh sin an aona bhó bhuamsa.

11. Gu ìre mo bhreacain guaille
. . . . . .

12. Sheadhain chridhe nan suilean mìogach
Cha tugainn a lagh no 'Righ thu.

13. Chuirinn eadar mi 's mo stìom thu
Chuirinn eadar mo dha chìch thu.

14. Eadar mi 's mo leine lìn thu
Eadar Brighid 's a bròg bhuinn duibh (?).

15. Cha tugainn a Mhoire mhìn thu
Ged thigeadh i 's a làmh sìnte.

16. 'S a Sheadhain 's a Sheadhain 's a Sheadhain
Sheadhain chridhe! nan sùl mìogach.

17. Chuirinn léine chaol an gilead ort,
Nighinn i 's a' bhùrn bu ghiorra dhomh.

18. Thiormaichinn air barr nam bioran i,
Nàile! Righ, dhianainn mire ris.

19. B' annsa Seadhan air cùl tobhta
Na mac righ 'na shìd air lobhtaibh.

20. Na faicte Seadhan ri bhuannachd
Chuirinn an crodh laoigh ga fhuasgladh.

21. Chuirinn an crodh dubh is ruadh ann
Chuirinn an léine thar m' uachdar.

22. Agus bùn an spàr mu chuailean,
Cha 'n eil bo dhubh no bo ghuailfhionn.

23. No bo-laoigh an iomall buaile
Nach cuirinn-sa a ghaoil ga d' fhuasgladh.

24. Chuir m 'athair mi a dh' àite carraideach.
An oidhche sin a rinn e banais dhomh.

25. S o chòn a Dhia nach b 'e m' fhalair i
Is bochd nach d' chuir e fo lic san talamh mi.

TRANSLATION.

1. Many have heard [the tale] who did not tell it (O hu ro, etc.) that my love had been in Minginish. (O hu hu ho hu ro, etc., etc.) 2. They said to me that I was a joyous woman ; a woman poor, mournful, in distress and sorrow am I. 3. O'er many a place have I wandered with thee ; I was in Alba and in Uist with thee. 4. I was in Erin, in Munster province with thee ; I heard mass in * Cill-Chumhaing with thee. 5. I was in Kildonan [in Eigg ?] in hiding with thee ; I drank a sip with thee in St. Cumhaing's Well. 6. I was in Islay ; I was in Uist with thee ; in Eriskay of the dark nooks. 7. Alas ! for such as·said to me that I was a joyous wife ; a wife unfortunate, tearful and sad am I. 8. Could Sedhan but be released, the trout would come [or be got] from the banks. 9. There would be neither black cow nor speckled cow in the lower nor in the upper part of the cattle-fold 10. that would not go in ransom of thee,—and that would deprive me of my one cow. 11. Even to the length of my shoulder-plaid (it would go to the ransom of Sedhan). 12. Sedhan ! heart's darling ! thou of the winning eyes, I would give thee neither to law nor king. 13. Between my snood [head-band] and me I would place thee, I would place thee between both my breasts. 14. Between me and my shirt of linen, between Brigit and her dark-soled shoon. 15. To the tender Virgin I would not give thee, even should she come with outstretched hand. 16. O Sedhan, O Sedhan, O Sedhan ! O darling Sedhan of the winning eyes. 17. I'd put a slender shirt full white on

* The singer said *Coill*=wood, hence "in the narrow wood," but it is a dialectal confusion for *Cill*. The saint's name I do not identify. It cannot be Cille-Chuimein (now Fort Augustus).

thee, I'd wash it in the burn-water next to me, 18. I'd set it on the stick-tops to dry ; in sooth, O King, I'd make merry. 19. Better [be with] Sedhan under shelter of a dyke than with king's son in silk in [a house with] wooden floor. 20. Could Sedhan but be seen and be got at, I'd give the calving-cows for his ransom. 21. The red cows and the black cows I'd give, I'd give the shirt off my back ; 22. the very stock of the house-joists in return for his locks [of hair] ; there is neither black cow nor brindled, 23. nor cow with calf in the side-stalls that I would not give in ransom of my beloved. 24. My father sent me to a place of difficulties the night he made me a wedding ! 25. Alas, O God, that it was not my funeral feast ! 'Twas pity that he did not put me in a grave underground.

Mrs. Mackellar's version concludes thus :

"If Sedhan would but arise again many a heart would be glad and rejoice. He was his godmother's darling, his wife's dear one, and a hidden lover was he unto me. Sedhan the high-souled, my pride and my joy, thou art low in thy winter dwelling, without the drinking of wine or of brandy, without the voice of song, or of music or dancing. Sedhan is to-night among the dead ; sad are the tidings to his followers. Glad are the tidings to the deceitful ones, bitter are the tidings to my heart. Better to be in my bed of earth than to be severed from him ; better to be in the bottom of the ocean than to hear of his death."

G. H.

I have noted a very close variant of this air, near Arisaig, in Inverness-shire, where it was formerly a favourite waulking-song.—L. E. B.

The tune is very similar in character to " Piobaireachd Dhomhnuill Dhuibh " (Pibroch o' Donald Dhu)—the regimental march of the Cameron Highlanders.—A. G. G.

52.—CHAIDH MIS' DH'AN TRÀIGH (i.).

(I WENT TO THE SHORE.)

Mode 3. *a.* (6-note scale.)   SUNG BY MARGARET GILLIES (COTTAR),
Slow   BRACADALE, ISLE OF SKYE, 1861.

52.—CHAIDH MIS' DH 'AN TRAIGH (ii.).

(I WENT TO THE SHORE.)

Mode 4. *b.* (6-note scale.)   SUNG BY OIGHRIG ROSS (COTTAR),
Moderate.   BRACADALE, ISLE OF SKYE, 1861.

1. Chaidh mis' dh'an tràigh 'S cha d 'rinn mi maor-ach, 2. 'S ged nach d 'rinn gu 'n d 'rinn mi caoin-eadh.

Hò rionn ò   hò   è   hò.   Hao ri ri o   è   hò.   Hò rionn ò   hò   è   hò.

In the first version, the verse is one line only, in the second a couplet (1 and 2).

TRANSLATION (Refrains indicated for Version i.).

(R. and Ch.) 1. I went to the shore at ebb-tide and gathered no shell-fish; (R. and Ch.) 2. and while I got none, I wept instead. 3. What a strange sight I beheld to-day 4. in the early morning when looking for sheep ! 5. A boat I saw going round the sandy beach. 6. Four were on board, and one person was baling; 7. a woman at the bow was calling aloud; 8. another woman at the stern was lamenting without cease; 9. and I enquired for what cause. 10. "It is not for the death of the year-old calves from leanness, 11. nor for the (thievish) sucking of the milk-cows, 12. but for my three brothers dead, and no more to be found. 13. I had climbed to the height above the cattle-fold, 14. and glancing over my shoulder observed 15. three men passing by, whom I supposed to be 'Duni-wassail' * 16. but who were only vulgar fellows; 17. and proceeding to the door of a cave, 18. where my brothers were lying in deep slumber, 19. they stabbed them with knives of steel, 20. their blood congealing in the rushes. 21. My own palms were cup for me, 22. conveying water to them from a cold pool, 23. sprinkling it upon their shoulders, 24. hoping that I might revive them. 25. But they neither moved nor turned."

I contributed both airs with Gaelic words to the *Gesto Coll.* (App. pp. 16 and 22).—F. T.

53.—COISICH A RÙIN !

(HASTEN THY PACE, BELOVED.)

Modes 2. *a.* and **1.** *a.* (6-note scale.)   SUNG BY MARGARET M'LEOD (COTTAR),
Slow.   PORTREE, SKYE, 1870.

1. Cois - ich,   a   rùin.   O   hù   ill o   rò   hò.   A   lùb   nan

* = gentlemen. (Lowland-Scottish form of the Gaelic "daoin' uasal.")

geal - làmh. Och hò rinn ò! Cois - ich, a rùin. O hi

ù ill ò rò hò! A lùb nan geal - làmh O hi ibh ò.

2. *Nan claidheamh geur
   'S nan arm gheala.

3. 'S minig a luigh
   Mi fo d'earradh.

4. Ma luigh cha b'ann
   Aig a bhaile.

5. Do làmh fo m'cheann
   'S d'aodach farum.

6. 'N lagan uaigneach,
   Cluaine bharraich.

7. Sloban nam beann
   Slor dhol tharruinn.

8. Is uisge fior-ghlan,
   Fuar-ghlan fallan.

9. Fo theang' an fhéidh
   A 's binne langan.

10. Is mis' a'bhean bhochd
    Th'air a cuaradh.

11. Bho'n thug na laoich
    Druim a chuan orr';

12. Luchd nan ròiseal,
    'S nan long luatha,

13. 'S nam brataichean
    Dearg is uaine.

14. 'S mis' a bhean bhochd
    Th'air a sgaradh;

15. Ma 'sè 'n cuan mór
    T'àite falaich;

16. Ma 'sè na ròin
    Do luchd-faire;

17. Ma 'sè leabaidh dhuit
    An fheamainn;

18. Ma 'sè cluasag dhuit
    A ghaineamh;

19. Ma 'sè na h'éisg do
    Choinnlean geala.

20. Tha sneachda mór
    Air na beannaibh.

21. Cha'n fhaigh Clann Nèill
    A dhol thairis.

22. Cha tig mo ghaol-sa
    Gu baile.

23. Nan cluinninn bean,
    Bhi'g a luaidh riut.

24. Spionainn bun
    Is barr mo chuailein.

25. Leumadh mo shròn
    'N àird na stuaidhe.†

26. Dh'fhalbhadh m'anail
    Na ceò uaine.

27. Shìninn mo chas
    Mar cheap uaghach.‡

*The words of each verse, sung solo to the first strain, are repeated as chorus to the second strain.

†*See* the *Macdonald Collection*, p. 259. "Leumadh mo shròn an àird na stuaighe," *i.e.* "My nose would flush up in anger."—G. H.

‡I have also heard "cheap tuathal" (a stumbling-block) sung instead of "cheap uaghach" (a slab over a tomb).—F. T.

1. Hasten thy pace, beloved, (R. : O hù, etc.) young man of the white hands, (K. : Och hò, etc. Ch.) 2. of the sharp swords, and of bright weapons! 3. Often have I lain beneath thy plaid, 4. but not at the homestead; 5. thy hand supporting my head, thy raiment covering me, 6. in a lonely hollow, a bower of foliage, 7. and the drift of the mountain passing over us. 8. Spring-water was there, pure, wholesome and cold, 9. beneath the tongue of the deer of most melodious bellowing. 10. A sad woman am I, who am in anguish 11. since the brave men have gone away over the sea; 12. they of bold exploits, of swift vessels, 13. and of banners red and green. 14. A mournful wife am I, and in distress 15. if thy hiding-place be the great sea, 16. if the seals be thy watch, 17. and thy bed the sea-ware; 18. if thy pillow be the sand, 19. and thy shining candles the fish! 20. There is deep snow on the mountains; 21. Clan Neill may not pass over, 22. nor my beloved reach home. 23. Were I to hear of another endearing herself to thee, 24. my hair I should pluck out by the root; 25. my nose would bleed forth in the height of my flush of anger, 26. and my breath go away in a green mist; 27. my feet I should stretch out like the top of a tomb.

I contributed this tune, without words, to the *Gesto Coll.* (App. p. 56). *See* the *Macdonald Collection* for another version of the song.—F. T.

The tune, with its character of restless longing, is well suited to the words. It seems to be a "repeating" tune, and is pentatonic in framework, though the 2nd degree, E, appears once. The 6th is absent.—A. G. G.

54.—HÓ RÓ, LAIL Ó.

PENTATONIC.
Mode 5.

SUNG BY MARY ROSS,
FROM KILLMALUAG, SKYE, 1900.

Hó ró, lail ó, ho ro hù ò, Ho hì na ho ro hù ò, Hó

ró lail o, ho ro hù ò! 1. Thàin - e tu-s' a Chuil-ein rùn - aich !

2. *Cha b'ionnan 's mar a dh'innseadh dhùinne.†
3. Gu'n robh thu'nad laigh an Diùrai ;
4. 'S gun do chàirdean a bhith dlùth dhuit ;
5. 'S do naimhdean bhith air do chùltbaobh ;
6. 'S nach robh fograich ann ad dhùthaich,
7. Ach daoine donna sheanga shunndach.

* Each verse-line is followed by the solo and chorus refrains.
† The accent is required here, for the music.

(R. and Ch.) 1. Thou art come, thou darling, (R. and Ch.) 2. and it was not as we were told ; 3. that thou hadst been ill in Jura, 4. having none of thy friends near thee, 5. while thy foes were in pursuit ; 6. and no outlaws in thy country-side, 7. but brown-haired, slender, and mirthful men.

As regards the tune, *see* note to "Cumha Mhic-Leoid," No. 43.—A. G. G.

55.—CUMHA BANTRAICH.

(A WIDOW'S LAMENT.)

PENTATONIC.

Mode 3.

SUNG BY MARY ROSS,
FROM KILLMALUAG, SKYE, 1900.

O! gur h-è mis' tha air mo leòn - adh! Hao - i o - ho,

O-ho i o - ho, Hao ri ri ù ò, Hao ri o - ho!

TRANSLATION.

Oh, how grievously am I afflicted ! (*Refrain* : Hao-i, etc. ; *Chorus* : Oho, etc.)

This was also used as a waulking-song.—F. T.

WAULKING SONGS.

MODERATE TEMPO TYPE.

56.—HUG Ó RIONN O.

Mode 3. *a* [with E♭]. (6-note scale.)

SUNG BY MARY ROSS
FROM KILLMALUAG, SKYE, 1900.

Hug ó rionn ó, cha taobh mi chlann ; Bho nach fhaod mi dhol 'nan cainnt. Hug ó rionn ó, cha

taobh mi chlann. 3. Ged chì mi chlann nigh-ean òg - a, Cha 'n fhaic mi do leith - id ann.

(Refrain: Hug ó rionn ó, I mix not with the young folk, *Chorus:* as I cannot use their speech. Hug o, etc. I mix not with the young folk.) 1. With weariness of heart I am overcome, dwelling on the Lowlanders' open plains. (S., R. and Ch.) 2. Though I behold the young women-folk, the delight of my heart is not with them. 3. Though I gaze on the young maidens, among them thy equal I do not see. 4. When I heard of thy betrothal, my head, I thought, would burst asunder. 5. When tidings of thy marriage came, better my funeral feast had it been!

See *Gesto Coll.* (App. p. 50), where, to a tune almost identical, I have contributed six Gaelic verses, of which five are translated here. The refrain precedes the first verse, and also follows every verse. The Gaelic verse given with the music is the third.—F. T.

57.—HÉ, MANND'* THU.

(AY, BASHFUL THOU.)

Modes 3 and 2. *a.*

Moderately slow.

2. †'N oidhche bha mi
   'N còir an locha;
   'N oidhche dhiùlt mi
   Fear a phoca.

3. C'àit am faic mi
   Fear a choltais;

4. Bho nach maireann
   Fionn no Osgar,

5. Torcul donn
   Gu cur cloiche

6. No Driuchd-Uaine
   Mac Righ Lochlainn?

† Interpolate the refrains, solo and chorus, as before, and begin every verse with the last two lines of the preceding.

TRANSLATION.

Refrain: Ay, bashful thou! 1. What a blunder · I committed · on that night · when I was near the loch;‡ (Ch.) 2. the night on which I refused him of the pouch! 3. When shall I see his equal

* G. *mannda* = lisping, stammering.

‡ The dots indicate the lines of the stanza, alternated with the refrain.

215

4. since Fionn and Oscar are not living, .5. Torquil the brown-haired to putt the stone, 6. nor Driùchd-Uaine, the King of Norway's son?

The name of Driùchd-Uaine is written according to the sound, without any attempt at translation. In Sinclair's *An t-Oranaiche* there is a poem with a refrain resembling that of the above song, and also in *Songs of the Hebrides*, edited by Mrs. Kennedy Fraser.—F. T.

"Hé, mannd' thu" is sometimes written "Heman Dubh," *i.e.* "Black Heman."
—G. H.

58.—AIR FÀIR AN LÀ.

(AT DAWN OF DAY.)

Mode 2. *a. b.* (7-note scale.)

SUNG BY MARY ROSS,
FROM KILLMALUAG, SKYE, 1900.

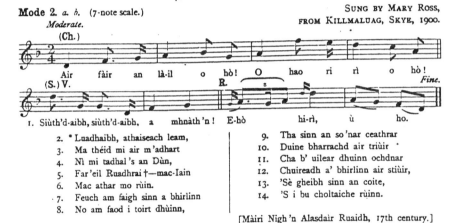

Air fàir an là-il o hò! O hao ri rì o hò!
(S.) V. R. E-hò hi-rì, ù ho.

1. Siùth'd-aibh, siùth'd-aibh, a mhnàth'n!

2. *Luadhaibh, athaiseach leam,
3. Ma théid mi air m'adhart,
4. Nì mi tadhal 's an Dùn,
5. Far 'eil Ruadhrai †—mac-Iain
6. Mac athar mo rùin.
7. Feuch am faigh sinn a bhirlinn
8. No am faod i toirt dhùinn,

9. Tha sinn an so 'nar ceathrar
10. Duine bharrachd air triùir
11. Cha b' uilear dhuinn ochdnar
12. Chuireadh a' bhirlinn air stiùir,
13. 'Sè gheibh sinn an coite,
14. 'S i bu choltaiche rùinn.

[Màiri Nigh'n Alasdair Ruaidh, 17th century.]

* The refrains, " Air fàir," etc., and " E-ho," etc., respectively precede and follow all the lines as in the first round.

TRANSLATION.

(*Chorus*: At dawn of day, o hò, etc.) 1. Begin, begin ye women, (*R*.: Eho, etc. ; *Ch.*: At dawn, etc.) 2. and waulk ye leisurely with me. 3. If I proceed on my way 4. I shall call at Dunvegan, 5. where Rory dwells, the son of Iain, 6. son of the father dear to me, 7. to try if we may get the galley, 8. or if he may give her to us [*literally*, "if she may be given to us"]. 9. We are here four in number, 10. one person more than three; 11. we should need to be eight 12. to put the galley on her course. 13. What we shall get is the fishing-boat, 14. which were more befitting for us.

[By Mary Macleod, 17th century.]

† Ruairi-Mór, 1600.

216

The incident commemorated in this waulking-song must have been of great importance at the time of its occurrence. For notes on Mary Macleod, *see* p. 262.—F. T. Bunting's air, "The Foggy Dew," has some likeness to this tune.—L. E. B.

59.—HÓ LEIB-A CHALL Ó.

Mode 4. *b.** (6-note scale.)

Moderate.

(S). R. V.

SUNG BY MARY ROSS, FROM KILLMALUAG, SKYE, 1899.

Hó leib - a chall ó. 1. Oidh - che bha mi'g fhair-e buail - e,

Hó leib - a chall ó. Dh'fhair-ich mi crith nach bu chrith fuachd i.

Hó leib hó ri hó ró hó. Hó leib - a chall ó.

Fine.

2. † Dh 'fhairich mi grìs nach bu ghrìs ruaidh i.
  Sùil dha 'n tug mi thar mo ghualainn,

3. Fear beag na feusaige ruaidhe,
  'Cìreadh 's a crathadh a ghruaige.

† The last line of each stanza is the first of the next.

TRANSLATION.

(*Refrain*: Ho leiba, etc.) 1. One night when watching the cattle-fold, (R.) I felt a shivering, which was not the tremor of cold; (Ch.) 2. and a shuddering I felt which was not the shuddering of "redness" [erysipelas]. On looking over my shoulder, 3. a small man I saw, whose beard was red, combing and shaking out his hair.

He was a fairy man who caused this horror and trembling to the person who was watching the fold by night. There is no further explanation of the incident, and the date of its occurrence is quite forgotten.—F. T.

This Gaelic working-tune should be compared with a Russian labour-air used, more especially, by raft-men of the Volga. The intervals and construction of both tunes are strikingly alike in many respects, and both, though primitive, have a singular pathos.—L. E. B.

* Or Mode 1. *b.*, if D be considered the tonic of this tune.—A. G. G.

217

RUSSIAN LABOUR-SONG.

60.—'ILLEAN Ò, RÒ MHAITH HÒ!

(O YOUTHS MOST EXCELLENT.)

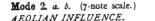

Mode 2. *a. b.* (7-note scale.)
AEOLIAN INFLUENCE.

SUNG BY MARY ROSS, FROM KILLMALUAG, SKYE.
EDINBURGH, 1907.

1. Hó! gur h-iad mo rùin na gill - ean! 'Ill - ean ò, ro mhaith ho! Dh 'iomr - adh 's a dh 'éigh-eadh iorr - am. E - hò l, hi ri ri ò! Hóg u ò! 'Ill - ean ò rò mhaith hò!

*Réidheadh null 's a nall throimh 'n Linne ;
'S ged a bhristeadh ràmh cha thilleadh ;
Ach fear eile 'chur 'na ionad.
Réidheadh a dh 'Eirinn ris a ghealaich,
Is thigeadh as ri aon seòl-mara.

Ho ! gur h-iad mo rùin na seòid,
Bha againn an raoir mu 'n bhòrd ;
Bha Mac-Coinnich ann 's Mac-Leòid,
Mac ic-Alasdair bho 'n t-Sròm,
'S Mac-Fhionghain o Shrath-nam-bò.

* Sung in couplets, the last line repeated to form the first of next stanza, with refrains interpolated.

TRANSLATION.

1. How much the lads delight me, (*Refrain* : O youths most excellent !) who, while they row, can sing aloud an "iorram." (Ch., R.) Who would traverse the waters † to and fro, and if an oar break, would not return, but put another in its place ; who would go over to Ireland by moonlight, and come again in one tide ! Oh, my pride is in the warriors whom we had last night at the board ; Mackenzie [of Kintail] was there, and Macleod [of Dunvegan, Harris, and Glenelg], Glengarry from Strome (-Ferry), and Mackinnon [of Strath] !

† ? Loch Linnhe.

See the *Macdonald Collection of Gaelic Poetry*, edited by the Rev. Angus Macdonald and the Rev. Archibald Macdonald (Inverness, 1911), p. 270, for another version of this song.—F. T.

This tune—one of the "endless" type—would seem to be founded on Mode 2, with Aeolian additions, but for one's feeling that the real *Fine* is on the semibreve B in bar 10, which note is equivalent to the tonic of Mode 4.—A. G. G.

I have a version of these words, sung to me by a very old crofter at Cross, Arisaig district, Inverness-shire, to an entirely different tune. *See* my note to "Hill-ean is ó hug ù," No. 66 in this Journal.—L. E. B.

61.—ORAN MU 'N GHRUAGAICH-MHARA.

(A SONG ABOUT THE MERMAID.)

Mode 4. *b.* (6-note scale.)

Moderate.

SUNG BY MRS. HECTOR M'KENZIE,
DUNVEGAN, SKYE, 1862.

Hill o ho, Hùill o ho. 1. 'S mis 'a chunn - aic! Hill o ho.

TRANSLATION.

(*Ch.* : Hill o ho, etc.) 1. What a wonderful sight (*R.* : Hill o, etc.) 2. I beheld to-day, 3. in the early morning when 4. I was searching for sheep! 5. A maiden I saw, 6. sitting on a rock alone, 7. and she had a grey robe 8. on for clothing. 9. It was not long ere 10. this changed ; 11. raising her head she stretched herself, 12. and assuming the appearance 13. of an animal without horns, 14. she went cleaving the sea on every side ; 15. through the Sound of Mull ; 16. through the Sound of Islay ; 17. through the Sound of Orasa 18. of Mac-Phee, 19. toward the spacious region 20. of the bountiful ones.

The above version, with Gaelic words, contributed by me to the *Gesto Coll.*, may also be found in *Puirt-a-beul* (1901), p. 45. (2nd set.) Tradition does not tell us the name of the spectator of this strange sight.—F. T.

The hornless animal * whose form the mermaid took, one may suppose to have been a seal. The "grey robe" of the maiden further points to her seal character, the seal being often described as "grey." "In the superstitious belief of the North," says Mr. W. T. Dennison in his *Orcadian Sketch-book*, "the seal held a far higher place

* *Cf.* also the "merrows" [moruadh = sea-maid ; *see* Shaw's Gaelic Dictionary, copied by O'Reilly] of Irish fairy tales, who sometimes come up out of the sea in the shape of "little hornless cows." When in their own proper form, the theft of their "diving-caps" will prevent their return to the sea. *See* "The Lady of Gollerus" in Yeats' *Irish Fairy Tales*, 1892.—A. G. G.

than any of the lower animals, and had the power of assuming the human form and faculties. .... Every true descendant of the Norsemen looks upon the seal as a kind of second-cousin in disgrace."* There are various "selchie" (seal) stories and ballads in Mr. R. M. Fergusson's *Rambles in the Far North*; among them a Breckness legend resembling the above song, which runs, briefly, thus: A young man beholds a beautiful maiden bathing in the sea, while beside her on a rock lies her slough or (seal-) skin. He obtains possession of the slough, thereby preventing, according to Orkney belief, her return to the water [note the analogy with swan-maidens], and wins her for his bride. In after years she regains possession of the hidden slough and returns to the ocean. The "spacious region of the bountiful ones" is evidently the open sea.—A. G. G.

62.—THOG AM BATA NA SIÙIL.
(THE BOAT HOISTED THE SAILS.)

Mode 3. *a.* (6-note scale.)
Moderate.

REMEMBERED FROM CHILDHOOD
IN MINGINISH, SKYE, 1848.—F. T.

1. Thog am bàt - a na siùil. Hi ri u ì u! Mach a Coll - a

gu Rùm. Hi ri u ì u! Hi ri ri u o, o - hi-ibh o, ho ro

hùr - ibh o ho ro! Mach a Coll - a gu Rùm. Hi ri u ì u.

2. O Uidhist a' bhrùc,
   Gu Hirt nan eun fionn.

3. Bha mo leannan-s' air a stiùir,
   Fear a's guirme dà shùil;

4. Fear a's gile cùl dùirn;
   Fear a's clannaiche cùl.

5. 'S truagh nach robh mi's mo ghràdh
   Air eilean mhara nach tràigh,

6. Gun bhàta, gun ràmh,
   Gun eòlas air snàmh.

* According to the Hebridean legend (*see* under "The Seal-Woman's Croon" in Mrs. Kennedy Fraser's *Songs of the Hebrides*) seals are "the children of the King of Lochlann under spells." Lochlann = Scandinavia, or, mythologically, "a wonderland beyond the seas."—A. G. G.

1. The boat hoisted the sails. (*K*. : Hi ri, etc.) out from Coll to Rum, (R., then Ch.) 2. thence to Uist of sea-ware, and St. Kilda * of white birds. 3. My beloved was at the helm, he of two eyes the most blue ; 4. the back of whose hand is most white, and the back of his head the curliest. 5. Oh, that my love and I were on an island of the sea without strand : 6. without boat, or oar, and with no knowledge of swimming !

I contributed this tune with almost similar Gaelic words to the *Gesto Coll.*—F. T.

63.—CHAIDH NA FIR A SGATHABHAIG.
(THE MEN HAVE GONE TO SCAVAIG.)

Mode 3. *b.* (6-note scale.)
Moderate.

REMEMBERED FROM CHILDHOOD
IN MINGINISH, SKYE, 1852.—F. T.

(S.)

1. Chaidh na fir a Sgath - abb-aig. Fà - ill ill, O - ho - ró :

V.

Tha 'n là 'n diu fuar ac'. O hi, ho - rionn o - hó,

(Ch.)

Hi ri rì ho - ro gù, Fàiil ill O - ho - ró.

2. Chaidh fear mo thighe-s' ann ;
   Caol mhala gun ghruaman :

3. Sealgair 'an ròin teillich thu ;
   Is na h-eilide ruaidhe ;

4. Is na circeige duinne thu,
   Ni a nead 's a luachair.

TRANSLATION.

1. The men have gone to Scavaig ; (*K*.: Fà ill, etc.) for them this day is cold. (*K*.: O hi ; *Ch*.: Hi ri.) 2. The goodman of my house went there : he of the slender eyebrows, showing no frown. 3. Hunter of the blub-cheeked seal art thou, and of the red hind. 4. and of the little brown hen that makes her nest among the rushes.

Contributed by me without translation to the *Gesto Coll.*—F. T.

Cf. " Hithil ùil agus ò," a Skye air, in Patrick M'Donald's *Highland Vocal Airs*,

* No Saint Kilda is known in the ecclesiastical year. Kilda is a word faked by the Dutch map-makers, and founded on a Norse word signifying "well, spring, fountain," applied to a sacred well on the island by the successors to the Viking settlers. The Gaelic to this day is Irt, h-Irt, Eilean h-Irt *or* h-Iort (without any saint's name), a word in Old Irish signifying "death."—G. H.

1781. I have noted an air (to other words), in Inverness-shire, which has a strong likeness to both the latter tune and the above.—L. E. B.

64.—AILEIN, AILEIN, 'S FHAD AN CADAL.

(ALAN, ALAN, LONG IS THY SLUMBER.)

PENTATONIC.
Mode 3.

SUNG BY OIGHRIG ROSS (COTTAR),
BRACADALE, SKYE, 1862.

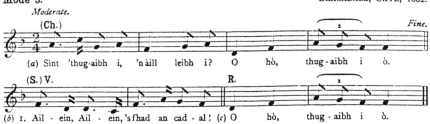

(a) Sìnt 'thug-aibh i, 'n àill leibh i? O hò, thug - aibh i ò.

(b) 1. Ail - ein, Ail - ein, 's fhad an cad - al! (c) O hò, thug - aibh i ò.

2. *Tha 'n uiseag 'gairm 's an là air glasadh.
3. Tha 'n ceò air sgaoileadh air an leacainn.
4. 'S fhad o 'n chàraich mi do leabaidh;
5. S cha b 'ann air lìc luim a chladaich;
6. Air clàiribh do luinge faide,
7. Tigh mór rùmail, ùrlar farsuinn.
8. Chunnacas bàta seach an rudha;

9. Chrath mi fhein mo bhreacan riuth';
10. Is dh 'ordaich mi bhi cuide riutha.
11. Gè nach b 'ann air ghaol am fuidheall,
12. Air gaol òg an òr-fhuilt bhuidhe.
13. 'Dhìreadh beann 's a theàrnadh bruthach,
14. 'Dh 'fhàgadh calp an fhéidh 'na spriùiribh,
15. Is eala bhàn nan spògan dubha.

* The lines come in in position (b) always preceded by (a) and followed by (c).

TRANSLATION.

(*Chorus*: † Reached forth, wish ye it? O-ho, give ye it !) 1. Alan, Alan, long has thy slumber been ! (*R.*: Oho, etc. ; then Ch.) 2. The lark is warbling, day has dawned, 3. and the mist has spread on the hill-side. 4. It is long since I have made thy bed ; 5. and not on the bare rocks of the sea-shore, 6. but on the boards of thy galley, 7. a spacious house with wide floor. 8. A boat was seen going round the headland, 9. and, waving my tartan scarf, 10. I wished that I might be with them ; 11. and not for love of their refuse [*or* "rubbish," *i.e.* the mean ones], 12. [but] for that of the youth of the golden hair 13. who climbs the mountain and descends the slope ; 14. who would leave the leg of the deer in fragments, 15. and the white swan with the black web-feet.

The above tune, with very similar Gaelic words, was contributed by me to the *Gesto Coll.* (App. p. 16).—F. T.

† Apparently a reference to the handing backwards and forwards of the cloth in waulking, as described in "A Singer's Memories of Life in Skye" in this Journal.

65.—CLÒ NAN GILLEAN.

(THE YOUNG MEN'S KELT, or CLOTH.*)

Mode 5. *b.* (6-note scale.)
Rather slow.

AS SUNG BY THE WAULKING WOMEN
AT RUDH'-AN-DÙNAIN, SKYE, 1850.—F. T.

1. "Cò chual - a ri - amh, Iom-air è hó!" "Clò nan Gill-ean, Iom-air è hó!"

"Ceòl bu bhinn - e, Iom - air è hó!" "Clò nan Gill - ean, Iom - air è hó."

2. No geum bà,
Chiar-dhubh chinn-dubh,

3. 'S iad 'g an teàrnadh,
Ri Strath-glinne?

TRANSLATION.

1. *Solo :* "Who ever heard—(Keep it going [*or* moving], ho !) "
Chorus : ("The young men's kelt, Keep it going, ho !")
Solo : "Music more melodious (Keep it going, ho !)"
Chorus : ("The young men's kelt, Keep it going, ho !")

2. *Solo :* "Than the lowing of kine (Keep it, etc.) "
Chorus : ("The young men's kelt, Keep it, etc.")
Solo : "Dark dun, and black their heads (Keep it, etc.)"
Chorus : ("The young men's kelt, Keep it, etc.")

3. *Solo :* "On their way down (Keep it, etc.)"
Chorus : ("The young men's kelt, Keep it, etc.")
Solo : "Down to Strath-glinne?"
Chorus : ("The young men's kelt, Keep it, etc.")

When B♮ is substituted, this air proves to be a variant of an Aeolian waulking-song to similar words noted by me near Loch Morar in Inverness-shire.—L. E. B.

66.—HILL-EAN IS Ó HUG Ù.

(THE CATTLE ARE LOWING IN THE PASTURE.)

PENTATONIC.
Mode 3.
Moderately slow.

SUNG BY MARY ROSS,
FROM KILLMALUAG, SKYE, 1901.

1. Tha 'n crodh a geum - naich 'san inn - is. Hill - ean is ó hug ù.

* "Kelt" = homespun.

(Ch.)

O - hó, hi ri ill ù ò, Hill - ean is ó hug ù.

(S.) V.
(Ch.)
Fine.

A dol a dh'itheadh feur na cill - e. O - hó, hi ri ill ù ò, Hill - ean is ó hug ù.

2. * 'S na laoigh bheaga 'gan iomain.
3. Ghaolaich, nach dean thu 'n tilleadh,
4. Gheibheadh tu na bha thu sireadh.

* In this song the last line (such as "A dol," etc., in the first verse) is repeated to form the first line of the next round, the refrains falling in the same positions as in the first verse. The (new) second line only of V. 2, 3, 4 is here printed.

TRANSLATION.

1. The cattle are lowing in the pasture, (*R.*: Hillean, etc.; *Ch.*: Oho, etc.) going to browse on the grass of the churchyard. (*Ch.*: Oho, etc.) 2. The little calves are being driven. 3. Dear, wilt thou not turn them? 4. Thou wouldst get what thou wast seeking.

I contributed a few lines to the version of this air in *Puirt-a-beul*, p. 11.—F. T.

The music of the last line of refrain resembles the last part of the Perthshire "Cattle-call" in Journal, vol. ii. p. 230.—A. G. G.

I have noted a close variant of this song in the Arisaig district of Inverness-shire, where it is used for waulking. The above text is, however, supplemented in my version by an opening line meaning "How sad am I, as I am being ill-used!" Then follows a similar text to the above, with the addition of words signifying, "If you do so you will get what you want of tartan put up to dry. You will get to lie in a dry blanket, and get a maiden with the full consent of her kindred." Upon this the singer grafted a full version of the words of the song, "'Illean o! ro mhaith, ho," see No. 60 in this Journal. *Cf.* the beginning phrase of "Ho ró mo chuid" in the *Gesto Coll.*, also "An Isle of Skye Dance" in *Albyn's Anthology*, p. 99.—L. E. B.

67.—SHIÙBHLAINN, SHIÙBHLAINN.

(I'D FOLLOW THEE, FOLLOW THEE.)

Mode. *See Note.*
Moderate, plaintive.

SUNG BY MARY ROSS,
FROM KILLMALUAG, SKYE, 1900.

(Ch.)

Shiùbhl-ainn, Shiùbhl-ainn, O hi ri u bhi. Dh'fhalbh-ainn fhein leat. O hi ri ibh.

(S.)

1. Rach-ainn throimh choill' ˙ O   hi ri u   bhi.   Dhlùth nan géug leat.   O   hi ri ibh.

2. Shiùbhlainn machair.
   Fada, réidh leat.

[Verses 1 and 2 * from Mary Ross of Killmaluag, Skye, 1900. The rest from Mrs. MacKinnon, Castlebay, Barra, 1902.]

3. Dh 'éirich mi moch,
   Maduinn Chéitein.

4. Dhìrich mi suas—
   Gual an t-sléibhe.

5. 'S chunna mi do
   Bhàt is bréid rith'

6. Sud am bàt a
   Chràidh 's a léir mi

7. Bhàthadh oirr' m'athair.
   'S mo thriùir bhràithrean.

8. Mo sheachd mollachd
   Aig na saoir,

9. 'Chuir giuthas innt'
   No chuir tàirnean.

10. Ach b'fhaide leam
    Am fear ghlac air làimh mi

11. Leathanach od'
    Bhonn gu d'bharr thu.

12. Sud mo dhìth
    Nach mi bha làimh riut.

13. Gè b'è sgeir, no
    Bodh an d'thràigh thu ;

14. Gè b'è tiurr an
    D'fhàg an làn thu.

15. Dh'òlainn deoch, gè
    B'oil le m'chàirdean ;

16. Cha'n ann dhe'n bhùrn,
    No dhe'n t-sàile,

17. Ach fuil do chuim, 's tu'n
    Déidh do bhàthadh.

TRANSLATION.

(*Chorus*: I'd follow, follow, Ohi ri u bhi, and go with thee, Ohi ri ibh.) 1. I'd go through forest (*R*.: Ohi ri, etc.) of dense branches (R. and Ch.) 2. and over plains wide and level. 3. I rose early one morning in May. 4. I climbed the mountain slope 5. and beheld thy boat with a sail. 6. That was the boat which caused me anguish. 7. My father was drowned in her, and my three brothers. 8. My seven-fold curse on the carpenter 9. who put pine in her, and nails ! 10. But greater my grief for him who had taken me by the hand. 11. A Maclean thou wert, from the sole of thy foot to thy crown. 12. Alas for me, that I was not with thee 13. on whatever reef or sunken rock thou wast stranded, 14. or on whatever beach the full tide left thee ! 15. I could drink—though displeasing to my kindred— 16. not of [fresh] water nor of brine, 17. but of thy body's blood after having been drowned.

In Barra, a variant of the lament on " Alan of the brown hair " is sung to the above tune. My version of the same air with a fragment of song is in *Puirt-a-beul*, p. 27.—F. T.

The words of the first verse and chorus of this song are incorporated in " Am

* These two opening verses do not seem to belong to the remainder.—A. G. G.

Fleasgach Donn" (The brown-haired Lad), No. 30 in the *Celtic Lyre*, from which fact it appears likely that "Shiùbhlainn, Shiùbhlainn," is an old refrain. *See* Mrs. Kennedy Fraser's *Songs of the Hebrides* for another version of the words under the title of a "Harris Love Lament (Ailean Donn)." Alexander Carmichael in *Carmina Gadelica*, vol. ii. p. 282, identifies the hero with a Captain Allan Morrison, drowned on his way to his marriage with Ann Campbell (daughter of Donald Campbell, the entertainer of Prince Charlie at Scalpay, Harris), who afterwards composed the lament. In Miss Tolmie's version, however, the drowned lover is described as a Maclean. Folk-lorists will note the allusion in the words to the barbaric custom of drinking the blood of a dead friend in token of affection.*

The present tune does not seem properly to belong to the song, and, as Miss Tolmie remarks, is ill-fitted to the tragic subject. It sounds like a country-dance, and is very similar in style to a tune attached to the children's game, "The rantin', tearin' Hielandman," or "The Tinker-leary Man," this also consisting of a 4-bar strain without any definite ending. The game-words are evidently connected with some older song lying behind the Scottish-Jacobite song of "The White Cockade," and the Irish "Shule agra" (the tunes of which two songs are also connected), the motive being a girl's declaration of her resolve to follow her beggarman or soldier through the world. In the game the words are, "I'll do all that ever I can To please my little Hielandman," or more commonly, "to follow my tinker-lairy" or "gable-oary [gaberlunzie] man." This old "shiùbhlainn" chorus—which suggests a connection with the Irish "Shule, shule" refrain—may have been originally merely a *port-a-beul*, more particularly as the tune here given seems to be a dance or marching tune. I feel some doubt as to the Gaelic origin of this tune, which seems more modern in structure than the rest of this collection.—A. G. G.

* Dr. Carmichael quotes verses from four distinct Gaelic songs referring to this custom, and reminds us that the poet Spenser relates how he saw a Limerick woman drinking the blood of her executed foster-son. Mrs. Fraser in a note on "Ailean Donn" tells us that Beathag Mor ("Big Bertha"), a poetess of Trotternish, Skye, drank "a mild intoxicating drink of the blood" of her lover, one Martin, tacksman of Duntulm, so late as the early years of the nineteenth century.—L. E. B.

WAULKING-SONGS.

FOR *WRINGING THE CLOTH.*

68.—ORAN TEANNACHAIDH.

(A SONG FOR TIGHTENING THE CLOTH.)

Mode 3. *a.* (6-note scale.)

In varying tempo.

SUNG BY MARY ROSS, FROM KILLMALUAG, SKYE, 1908.

Seinn * O !   hur-aibh i   ibh   O !   1. Chaidh mi 'na Ghleann-an a's t-Fhogh-air.

(Ch.)

Seinn   O ! ho ro,   hur-aibh i   ibh   O !   Thilg mi na cruinn is f huair mi 'n tagh-adh.

2. † Fhuair mi 'n t-òg-fhear seòlta seadhach, }
3. Òganach gun tòir 'na dhéidh. } (Verse 3.)
4. Theid thu 'n a' bheinn am bi 'mheaghail,
5. Le do mhial-choin, gheala-choin sheadhach,
6. 'S le do choin bheag as an déidh.
7. Sud mo leannan, 's cha b 'fhear fuadain,
8. 'S cha bu lurg bhreac o luath e
9. 'S cha bu ghlasneulach bho 'n fhuachd e.
10. Sud mo leannan, Gille-Calum,
11. Sud mo leannan Calum gaolach,
12. Fear beag aotrom uallach, ùiseil
13. Théid thu 'n a 'bheinn am bi 'n aonaich ‡
14. Thoirt nan uibhean as na fraochaibh.
15. 'S cha bhitheadh mo chuids' dhiubh gun fhaotainn.
16. A broilleach do leine caoile.

† In this song the last line of each verse is repeated to form the first verse-part of the next round. The new second line only of each verse is here printed.

TRANSLATION.

(*R.*: Sing O, hurivivo.) 1. In autumn I went to the Little-Glen ; (*Ch.*: Sing O, etc.) I cast lots, and won the best. (*R.*: Sing O.) 2. A young man I found, clever and wise ; 3. a youth after whom there was no pursuit. 4. Thou goest to the hill, where barking is heard, 5. with thy greyhounds, thy sagacious white dogs, 6. and thy terriers following them. 7. Such is my beloved, and no wanderer,

* *i.e.* "Sing O hur-iv-i-iv-o ! "   ‡ *Dialectal for* "àinich."

8. nor one whose legs are mottled at the fireside; 9. nor a person rendered pale from cold. 10. Such is my lover, Gille Calum, 11. such my lover, Calum dear. 12. His figure is slight; he is proud, and respected. 13. Thou goest up the mountains panting, [*literally*, "where will be the panting",] 14. to gather the eggs among the heather; 15. and my share doubtless will be forthcoming 16. from the bosom of thy linen shirt.

"Tightening" the cloth; that is, wringing it till the moisture was nearly absorbed, was the last process of waulking, accompanied by a song like the above, in a varying measure, expressive now of leisure, and now of urgent haste. The following snatch (meaning "Ho! Well done! with noise! Ho! Bravo, the cloth!") was sung with this varying speed at the close of a waulking. About a hundred and twenty years ago, Donald Gillies of Bracadale, when a herd-boy, was resting one summer's day on a grass-grown fort near Caroy. Laying his head on the sod, he distinctly heard the fairies waulking beneath, and shouting heartily:

HÓ, FIREAM, FORUM.
(A SONG FOR TIGHTENING THE CLOTH.)

Mode 3. *b.* (6-note scale.)

Hó,　　fir - eam　for - um　　foirm;　　Hó,　　fair - eag - an,　an　clò!

Some of the songs of slow measure were sung whilst the cloth, duly fulled and washed, was wound round a piece of wood called the "coinneal," preparatory to being pressed.—F. T.

69.—IÙ RI RIBH O!

Mode 2. *a.* (6-note scale.)
In varying tempo.

SUNG BY MARY ROSS,
FROM KILLMALUAG, SKYE, 1908.

(Ch.) R.

I　　ù　　ri ribh ó!　I　　ù　　ri ribh ó!

(S.) V.　　　　　R.　　　(Ch.)R.

1. Fir-e fair - e! ruag - air - e! Hi'm bó ha!　I　ù　ri ribh ó,　I　ù　ri ribh ó!

228

(S.) V.   R.

2. Gaol an gurr-ach anns a'ghart.   Fir - e   fair - e! ruag - air - e! Hi'm   bó   ha!

3. 'S docha leam an dùbhradh ud   4. Cas air ulaidh dhuit a ghràidh,
   Na mo thriùir mac.   Fire, faire! ruagaire!
                                            Hi'm bó ha!

                    5. Innsidh tu-s' a sud,
                       A phiseag ghlas.

TRANSLATION (without refrains).

1. "Ay, ay! [What a to-do!] Thou who dost pursue! 2. Dear to me is the queer figure in the cornfield. 3. That object in the distance I prefer to my three sons. 4. Foot on treasure for my dear. 5. This" [sung very slowly] "thou wilt go and repeat," [sung in a hurried manner] "thou grey kitten!"

This song was sung while wringing the cloth. Probably originally an old dancing-song, it is now chiefly used when dandling children. The words sung in refrain (perhaps a better word than "chorus" in this case) are meaningless. The story attached to the song is as follows: There was once a very old woman who had a treasure in a hidden place which she could not be persuaded to reveal to any one. Her sons at last bethought them of a means to discover her secret by making her believe that a scarecrow, which they had set up in a cornfield and moved about among the ricks, was a lover who had come to peep at her but dared not approach nearer. She was so pleased with this notion that one day, when her sons were concealed and listening to her words, she set her foot on the very spot where she kept the hoard for the benefit of her supposed admirer. Then observing that the young cat had followed her, and was certain to have overheard all that she had been saying, she exclaimed: "This thou wilt go and tell, thou grey kitten!" After that, no one annoyed her any more about the treasure, and the lover was forgotten.—F. T.

Cf. the Irish tune, to modern words, "The return from Fingal," in Stanford's *Songs of Old Ireland.*—L. E. B.

This tune appears to me distinct in character from any other in this collection, and is perhaps of Norse origin. It is reminiscent of Norse and other sailor-songs (*cf.* a version of "Haul the Bowline," in the same gapped mode, in *Old Sea Chanties*, edited by Bradford and Fagge), and a Gaelic friend confirms my belief that the refrain, "Hi'm bó ha," is "not Gaelic." These words * may be a corruption of some chanty-chorus, such as "Heave, my boys, haul!" or a similar refrain. The Norse equivalents for "heave" and

* May not some nonsense-refrains in Gaelic songs be corruptions of the syllables used in *canntaireachd*, the system whereby pipers preserved and transmitted their music?—F. T.

229

"haul" would not differ much in sound from the English. There are other evidences, in this collection, of Norse intercommunication or influence, not extraordinary when one considers the abundant relics of Norse settlement found in the speech, pronunciation, and place-names of the more northerly islands, Orkney and Shetland.—A. G. G.

WAULKING-SONGS.

IMPROVISATORY TYPE.

70.—AN LONG ÉIREANNACH.

(THE IRISH SHIP.)

Mode 1. *b.** (6-note scale.)

Moderate.

SUNG BY MARY ROSS,
FROM KILLMALUAG, SKYE, 1900.

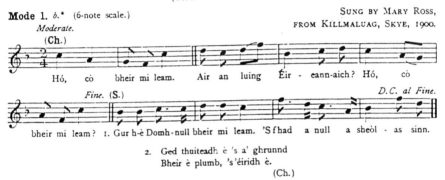

Hó, cò bheir mi leam. Air an luing Éir - eann-aich? Hó, cò

bheir mi leam? 1. Gur h-è Domh-null bheir mi leam. 'S fhad a null a sheòl - as sinn.

2. Ged thuiteadh è 's a' ghrunnd
Bheir è plumb, 's 'éiridh è.
(Ch.)

TRANSLATION.

(*Chorus*: Ho! whom shall I take with me on board the Irish ship? Ho! whom shall I take with me?) 1. It is Donald I will take, and we shall go far under sail. (Ch.) 2. Though he should tumble into the depths of the sea, he will plunge, and rise again.

The above waulking-song, being improvised, gave opportunity for the production of absurd and witty rhymes bearing on the association of the name of one of the young men in the audience with that of some woman elderly or young, who, singing non-sensical and extravagant words in his praise and working him up in the cloth, as it were, was in this manner to lift him out of the tub into which he was supposed to have fallen, and to bear him away with her on board the imaginary Irish ship. See *An Duanaire*, p. 121.—F. T.

* C has been taken as the tonic of this tune in classifying it.—A. G. G.

71.—'CHRAOBH AN IUBHAIR.

(O YEW TREE.)

Mode 4. *a. b.* (7-note scale.)

Moderate.

(S.) R.

SUNG BY MARY ROSS,
FROM KILLMALUAG, SKYE, 1908.

'Chraobh   an iubh - air,   hóg   u   ò!   Hi-ùr - aibh   o

ho   ro   lèath - ag - aidh!   'Chraobh   an   iubh - air,   hóg   u   ò.

1. Tog - aidh, tog - aidh mi   mo ghràdh.   'Chraobh   an iubh - air, hóg   u   ò.

2. Fada, fada os cinn chàich. (R. and Ch.)
3. 'S maith an t-iomainich air blàr. (R. and Ch.)
4. Caman òir an làimh mo ghràidh. (R. and Ch.)
5. 'S am ball airgid air an làr. (R. and Ch.)

TRANSLATION.

(*Refrain*: O yew-tree, etc. *Ch.*: Hiùraibh, etc.) 1. My beloved I will raise, I will raise (R. and Ch.) 2. Far, far above the others. 3. Excellent player on the field; 4. A club of gold in his hand, 5. And a silver ball upon the ground.

A fragment of one of the ridiculous songs, imagining the rescue of some favoured youth from the waulking-tub, and the distinction conferred upon him above all other men. The meaning of the refrain is no longer remembered by persons with ordinary knowledge of ancient lore.—F. T.

A song in the characteristic rhythm of the old nursery-song "Brochan buirn"—a version of which tune I have noted, at Loch Awe, to the modern song "Cruachan-Ben." The compass of "'Chraobh an Iubhair" suggests the Mixolydian mode, though the *Fine* is upon the Dorian tonic. Dr. Joyce's tune "The Yew Tree," No. 194 in his *Old Irish Folk Music*, has no connection with this.—A. G. G.

72.—GOIRIDH AN COILEACHAN UAIR ROIMH LÀ.

(THE COCK WILL CROW AN HOUR BEFORE DAY.)

SUNG BY MARY ROSS,
FROM KILLMALUAG, SKYE, 1908.

Mode 3. *b*. (6-note scale.)

Moderate.

Goir-idh an coil-each-an uair roimh là. Goir-idh an coil-each-an
uair roimh là. 1. Ru-air-i òg a tigh-inn 'na bhail-e so! Goir-idh an coil-each-an
uair roimh là. Goir-idh an coil-each-an uair roimh là. Cò i a 'ghruag-ach
bheir è o'n chag-ail-te? Goir-idh an coil-each-an uair roimh là.

2. * Gur h-i Seònaid bheir è o 'n chagailte.
3. Cò an gille theid ga tilleadh air?
4. Gur h-è Domhnull théid ga tilleadh air,

5. 'S bheir è a stigh i 'n làthair a' Mhinisteir,
6. 'S bheir è pòg, is rùn a chridhe dh 'i.

* The last line of each verse is repeated to form the first verse-line of the following round.

TRANSLATION.

Refrain: The cock will crow an hour before day. (Repeat as Ch.) 1. Young Rory is coming to this hamlet. (R. and Ch.) Who is the maiden whom he will take from the hearth? (R. and Ch.) 2. Janet is she whom he will take from the hearth. 3. Who will go and turn her from him? 4. Donald will go and turn her from him. 5. And will lead her into the Minister's presence 6. And give her a kiss, and the love of his heart.

This is a song the words of which are improvised to suit the above tune and sung with great merriment, the names of persons present being mentioned and amusing announcements made according to the wit of the singer. It is supposed that the cock predicts each piece of news in the early morning. If the feet of the cock be warm, a marriage may soon be expected; if cold, the omen is of sorrow.—F. T.

Dr. Maclagan, in his *Games and Diversions of Argyleshire*, gives a specimen of a similar waulking, or spinning-party dialogue—"Co Fear," or "Cuir a mach Leannain."

In Dr. Maclagan's version, the cock crowing *twice* seems to have been the omen of a marriage. These improvised game-songs may be compared with the Irish "loobeens," for an account of which, *see* Bunting and Petrie.—A. G. G.

73.—HÓ RÓ, THÙGAIBH I.

(HÓ RÓ, GIVE IT YE!)

Mode 5. *b*. (6-note scale.)

Moderate.

SUNG BY MRS. MACLEAN (CROFTER'S WIFE), CASTLEBAY, BARRA, 1902.

[Uist singer.]

1. Cha téid Mór a Bharr - aidh bhròn - ach. Hó ró, thùg - aibh i.

An d'thùg-aibh dh'is', an d'thùg - aibh éil - e. Hó ró, thùg - aibh i.

2. * Cha téid Catrion' ann le deòin.
    S.R.: Hó ró, thùgaibh i.
    Ch.: An d'thùgaibh, etc.
3. Cha téid Una, cha téid Seonaid,
4. No Anna ged is i as òige.
5. Cha b'è mo thìr-s'an tìr bhrònach :
6. Fàsaidh peasair, 's fàsaidh pònair ;
7. Fàsaidh corc ann, 's fàsaidh eòrna ;
8. 'S fàsaidh lion 'na chruachan òr-bhuidh.

9. 'S gheibheadh Eireannaich an leoir innt'.
[Barra singer.]
10. 'S fhada mi'm chadal 's mi diomhair,
11. 'S ma dhùisgear, gur garbh mo chiocras,
12. 'G éisteachd bleideag na Ròdhaich.
13. C'uim nach d'fhoighneachd am bu bheò mi ?
14. Bradag nan obag, 's nan òisinneag,
15. Chuireadh na luingis air seòladh.
16. Gu mullach nam beanntan móra.

* Every line is a verse, followed by a refrain, that of solo first, and then that of chorus.

TRANSLATION.

[Uist singer.] 1. "Mor will not go to miserable Barra (*S.R.* and *Ch.*: Ho ro, give it ye, etc. †), 2. nor will Catriona, with her consent ; 3. Una will not go, nor Janet, 4. nor Ann, though she be the youngest. 5. Not like my country is this wretched land ; 6. peas will grow there, and barley, 7. and flax in golden yellow heaps ; 8. the land of eating, and the land of drinking, 9. where the Irish might be satisfied with as much as they could wish !" (etc.). [Barra singer.] 10. "Long have I been as if asleep and retired ; 11. but if roused, vehement will be my desire, 12. listening to the impertinent woman of the Munroes ! 13. Why was I not asked if I were alive ? 14. The mischievous woman practising tricks of witchcraft, 15. who would set vessels sailing 16. on the tops of the great hills !"

Many generations ago, there was a great waulking in Barra for the Chief of Clan Neill, who was then residing at Kismul Castle, situated on a rock in Castlebay. Two

† See footnote to refrain in No. 64.

bardesses who were present had a contest in song as to the merits of their respective countries, the one being a native of Barra and the other from Uist. The singers indulged in vituperation which was mistaken for wit, and the Barra woman finally gave her opponent such fierce and painful word-thrusts that she fell forward on the waulking-board and died in consequence.* In Skye there is a tradition that Mary Macleod, the celebrated poetess, was there, and was not silent. The above lines are but a small portion of the original song.—F. T.

REAPING SONG.

USED ALSO FOR WAULKING.

74.—ORAN ARABHAIG.

(A SONG OF STRIFE.)

PENTATONIC.
Mode 3-5.

SUNG BY MARGARET GILLIES (COTTAR), EBOST, BRACADALE, SKYE, 1863.

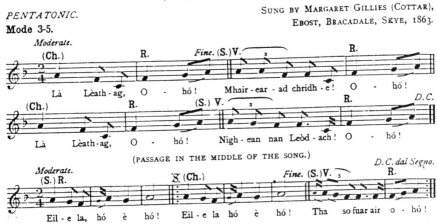

(PASSAGE IN THE MIDDLE OF THE SONG.)

TRANSLATION (without refrains).

(*Chorus*: Là Lèathag, Ohó!) [Macdonald poetess speaks:] "Margaret dear, (R., Ch., R.) daughter of the Macleods, (R.) with yellow hair of golden hue, the year of thy marriage seems long gone by.... Once, when I was sitting near the Sound of Rona, my face turned towards Hirt [St. Kilda] of big birds, a fellow came, boastful and pert, in velvet dress, with boots and spurs, and asked me—desiring conversation—what

* For an Irish illustration of the deadly effects of bardic satire *see* "Seanchan the Bard" in Yeats' *Irish Fairy Tales.* The hungry bard's egg having been stolen by mice, he satirises the whole tribe so venomously in a bardic chant that ten mice drop dead in his presence!—A. G. G.

234

was the custom with Clan Donald—well-known to me, befitting them: wine flowing; ale of third drawing poured from flagons. Not such as they, the race of Macleod, the race of the Mare, crippled and clumsy; feeding on chaff and coarsest grass, and black mill-dust; devouring barley with soft water from the peat-bog, greeted only as 'Pru-seò-i,' * with halters fastened round their heads, and withies upon their feet!" [Macleod poetess speaks:] "Come! Çome! Ye fled away, ye timid rabble! Remember ye the day of Glen-Healtuinn? Ye stood in the heather like hens; into the loch ye went like ducks, and like the gulls went out to sea!" [Macdonald poetess speaks, to Tune ii.:] (*Solo Ref.*: Eile la, etc. *Ch.*: Eile la, etc.) "This is intolerable (Ch.) and tedious! · Unpleasant is the talk that · may not be told · in the presence of Macleod · when at dinner!" (Ch.) [Tune i. is resumed. Macleod poetess speaks:] "What may yonder vessel be, inside the bend of the shore?" [Macdonald poetess speaks:] "Lo! the galley of Donald Gorm of the Isles! Having left this and the other headlands behind, she knocked a board off the galley of MacKenzie (of Kintail) out-running the galley of Macleod." [Macleod poetess speaks:] "Were it not for my heart failing, and weakness of voice from little strength, a true recital could I sing to the men down there at Dunvegan of numerous ships. It is Rory † who has the grand galley that goes to Islay and to Arran, young men drinking on her sarking" [*i.e.* the inner lining of thin boards in a ship].

[The second tune in the foregoing song is sung thus: First the Solo Ref., then Ch., followed by six solo lines each ending with Ch. Then the first tune is resumed and sung as before, with the difference that, at starting, "La Lèathag Ohó" is given out *solo* before being sung in Ch. The dots represent the recurring Ch. which punctuates the six solo lines.]

The Song of Strife, sung when reaping or waulking, is commemorative of the feud between Donald Gorm Macdonald, of Sleat, and Rory Mor Macleod of Harris and Dunvegan, in 1601. Two women hailed one another from each side of the Snizort river which formed a boundary between the territories of Macleod and Macdonald, and gave expression to their sentiments in the above manner. On a day in harvest, more than a hundred years ago, when every sort of outdoor work was accompanied by songs of suitable rhythm, a party of reapers assembled at Ebost, in Bracadale, divided themselves into two rival bands representing the poetesses who had originally sung the words of strife, and, while working with all their might to be first at the other end of the field which they were reaping, sang this song with so much fervour that they unconsciously cut themselves with their sickles and had very sore hands at the close of day. I contributed the tunes with Gaelic words to the *Gesto Coll.* (App. p. 53). The melody of the middle passage bears a strong resemblance to the cadence in the voice of a Gaelic preacher when greatly moved by the subject of his discourse to a sympathetic audience. The allusion to the horse or mare ("the race of Macleod—the race of the Mare") is explained by a friend: The Macleods who fought and were defeated on the day of Glen Healtuinn must have been not of the Skye or Harris branch, but of the Macleods of Raasay and Lewis, whose emblem or totem was the horse. If a person were to have a dream about a "grey horse" he was sure to have dealings soon with a Lewis man, for good or ill.—F. T.

---

* *i.e.* like horses being called.   † Rory Mor Macleod, 1600.

ROWING SONGS ("IORRAIM").

USED ALSO FOR WAULKING.

75.—IÙRAIBH O-HÌ, IÙRAIBH O-HÙ.

SUNG BY OIGHRIG BEATON (COTTAR),
BRACADALE, SKYE, 1863.

Mode 5. *a.* (6-note scale.)

Slow.

I - ùr - aibh o - hì,   iùr - aibh o - hù. 1. Chì mi'n t-àit''s an robh mi'n

uir - idh,   hó rò ho - ì,   O - ho eil - e.

TRANSLATION.

(*Chorus*: Iùraibh, etc.) 1. The place I behold, where last year I was staying, (*R.*: Hórò, etc.) 2. though this year I no longer there abide; 3. the slopes of Lochiel and of Kinloch-Luinnard, 4. Kinloch of the vessels and of fleets. 5. On Saturday I was seized with sorrow, 6. and never have been so overcome; 7. sitting solitary on the knoll, 8. where I could not hear the voice of any other person; 9. hearing the sound of the waves; 10. the rustle of the hazel against the holly, 11. of the sand-drift over the sea-bent, 12. of the nut-trees against the moss, 13. the stir of the foreigners and their ships, 14. the noise of the ropes against the blocks, 15. and the sound of oars rending the waves. 16. How sorrowful I am! 17. No boat can I behold, nor skiff 18. sailing from the land of the bent-grass, 19. returning from the land of the billows [Uist]. 20. I see the deer on the moor, 21. and the geese lingering on the strand. 22. They may remain there safe from harm ; 23. my hunts-man will not shed their blood. 24. My brown-haired sportsman lies enfolded, 25. and the chest of boards is fastened. 26. When I see the men passing along 27. I make no choice among them. 28. Beloved by me was the genial hero, 29. who grew not up sluggish, weak, nor indolent; 30. was never drunken at the beer-house. 31. A greatly afflicted woman am I ; 32. John have I buried, 33. and Ruairi, the brown-haired youth, his locks in curls, 34. at the temple on the hill.

This was a rowing as well as a waulking-song. The movement being slow, it was suitable when a boat was well-laden and heavy. The tune, with the Gaelic words contributed by me, may be found in *Puirt-a-beul*, p. 47.—F. T.

The slow and solemn character of several of these rowing-measures appears in some instances to be due to the fact that they were also of the nature of laments, being chanted by the rowers conveying the remains of chiefs across the western seas to Iona. (*See* Pattison's *Gaelic Bards.*) Mrs. Kennedy Fraser has an arrangement of this song, under the title "Sea-Sounds," in her *Songs of the Hebrides*, as noted from Miss Tolmie's singing.—A. G. G.

76.—EILE NA HURAIBH O-HO.

Mode 3. *a.* (6-note scale.)
Moderate.
(S.) R.
‎Ȿ (Ch.)
SUNG BY MARY ROSS,
FROM KILLMALUAG, SKYE, 1898.
Fine. (S.) V.
R.

Eil - e na hùr - aibh o - ho! Eil - e na hùr - aibh o - ho! 1. 'S fiuch an oidh - che, o

(Ch.) (S.) V. R. *D.C. dal Segno.*

hù, a - hó. Eil - e na hùr-aibh o - ho.'Nochd 's gur fuar - i! o - hùr - aibh o - ho.

Solo : 2. Thug an iùbhrach, o-hù, a-hó
   Chorus : Eile na hùraibh, o-ho
Solo : Ùr an cuan oirr', o-hùraibh, o-ho. (Ch.)

3. Dùrachd slàn dh'an
   T-saor a dh'fhuaigh i.

4. Dh'fhàg è dionach
   Làidir, luath i.

5. Acfhuinneach gu
   Siubhal chuanta.

6. Cha 'n eil bòrd fliuch innt',
   No bòrd fuaraidh.

7. 'S ioma sgeir dhubh
   Ris 'na shuath i ;

8. Agus faochag
   * Chròm a ghluais i.

9. Cha 'n 'eil cùram
   Orm m 'a fuadach ;

10. Tha mo rùn air
   Bòrd a fuaraidh.

11. Làmh cheangail nam
   Ball 's 'gam fuasgladh.

12. Cha b 'è fear cearraig
   Bheireadh bhuat e ;

13. No fear laimhe-
   -Deis' is fuachd air.

TRANSLATION.

Solo Ref. : Eile na, etc. (Repeat in Ch.) 1. The night is rainy, (Ch.) and it is also cold. (Ch.) 2. The new ship has turned towards the ocean. 3. My blessing be with him who built her, 4. and left her secure, strong and swift, 5. well-equipped for traversing the seas. 6. There is not a wet nor damp board in her, 7. and she has swept close by many a black rock, 8. moving the lowly whelk. 9. I have no fear lest she be driven out of her course, 10. for my beloved is on her windward side, 11. whose hand fastens the ropes and loosens them. 12. Not a left-handed man is he to take the helm, 13. nor his the right hand of a man benumbed with cold.

In the rhythmic rise and fall—the ocean swing—of its well-marked choruses, this song possesses considerable resemblance to a sea-chanty, and was perhaps originally one of the working-songs of the sea.—A. G. G.

237

77.—O HI IBH O.

(GREETING ACROSS THE SEA.)

Mode 4. *a. b.* (7-note scale.)
Rather slow.

SUNG BY MARY ROSS,
FROM KILLMALUAG, SKYE, 1898.

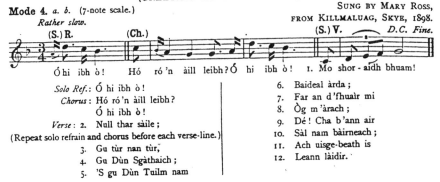

Ó hi ibh ò!　Hó　ró 'n　àill leibh? Ó　hi　ibh ò!　1. Mo shor - aidh bhuam!

Solo Ref.: Ó hi ibh ò!
Chorus: Hó ró 'n àill leibh?
Ó hi ibh ò!
Verse: 2. Null thar sàile;
(Repeat solo refrain and chorus before each verse-line.)
3. Gu tùr nan tùr,
4. Gu Dùn Sgàthaich;
5. 'S gu Dùn Tuilm nam

6. Baideal àrda;
7. Far an d'fhuair mi
8. Òg m'àrach;
9. Dé! Cha b'ann air
10. Sàl nam bàirneach;
11. Ach uisge-beath is
12. Leann làidir.

TRANSLATION.

(*R.*: Ó hi, etc.　*Ch.* Hó ró 'n, etc.) 1. A greeting from me (R. and Ch.) 2. across the sea 3. to yon tower of towers; 4. to Dun Sgathaich, 5. and to Duntulm 6. of the lofty battlements, 7. where I was reared 8. in childhood, 9. and truly not on 10. brine of limpets, 11. but on whisky 12. and strong ale!

This song, though an "iorram" (rowing-song), was sometimes raised at a waulking. Dun Sgathaich and Duntulm, two ancient strongholds, are situated at the northern and southern extremities of the Macdonald territory in the island of Skye.—F. T.

78.—ORAN DO DHOMHNULL GORM.

(A SONG TO DONALD GORM.)

PENTATONIC.
Mode 2.
Slow.

SUNG BY HARRIET M'VICAR (SPINNER),
NORTH UIST, 1870.

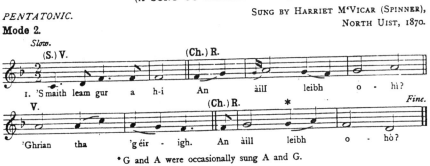

1. 'S maith leam gur　a　h-i　An　àill　leibh　o - hì?

'Ghrian　tha　'g éir - igh.　An　àill　leibh　o - hò?

* G and A were occasionally sung A and G.

238

1. I rejoice that it is she, (* *Chorus Ref.*: Is it your will, o-hì?) the sun, which is rising (*Ch.R.*: Is it your will, o-hò?), 2. and dimness passing over the stars. 3. The son of my king [Macdonald of the Isles] rrays himself ; 4. a hundred sitting beside thee ; a hundred standing round ; 5. a hundred to play the foot-ball for thee. (*The song proceeds* :) Wish ye the might of victory, ye heroes of the Feinn ? When the son of my king takes his course in due order,† may the vigour of Cu-Chulainn be with him ; the power of the Feinn ; the energy of little Ossian, and of Oscar the strong ; the energy of the brown stag that springs on high ; the strength of the sea, of weight and power ; the strength of the world be thine, and the strength of the sun. May Brian ‡ be to thee what I am to thee ; for like a full sister am I to thee, and if not more, certainly as much. . . . Numerous as are the leaves on the thorn-tree, or the yellow-headed sheaves on a harvest-field, so at the court of Donald are shields and swords ; and at the court of Donald are valiant men, etc.

Donald Gorm was Chief of Clan Donald in the reign of James VI., 1603, and a contemporary of Rory Mor Macleod, with whom he had a feud resulting in raids and fierce combats among their followers, while the devoted foster-mothers fanned the flames of wrath with passionate songs. This poem by the foster-mother of Donald Gorm may be found in *The Gael*, a Gaelic magazine which was in circulation for a few years (1870–1880). In his forthcoming volumes (iii. and iv.) of *Carmina Gadelica*, Dr. A. Carmichael will include the Gaelic words of the above in complete form. It was originally sung as an "iorram" (rowing song), but became eventually a waulking-song ; and is now only remembered by a small number of elderly persons.—F. T.

The tune is very characteristic (especially in its opening and closing phrases) of the Western Highlands. I have noted a very similar air there to the words, "Tha mi trom's duilich leam," which also ends with the drop from keynote to sixth.—L. E. B.

Is this "iorram," in the Scottish pentatonic scale, a simple and short form of the air called "The Irish Hautboy" in the *Petrie Coll.*, 1855? The "Irish Hautboy" ends in the major (corresponding to the note F in the "Donald Gorm" tune), and on comparing the two tunes it seems doubtful whether the last note, D, of Miss Tolmie's tune does not belong as much to the beginning as the end, forming a linking-note between each repetition.—A. G. G.

* See note on a similar refrain to No. 64.

† In due order = *deiseal*, the way of the sun, from east to west.

‡ Brian, properly one of the gods of Celtic heathendom. See *Survivals in Belief among the Celts*, George Henderson (MacLehose, Glasgow, 1911).

MILKING SONGS.

79.—THA 'N CRODH AIR NA LÒIN.
(THE CATTLE ARE ON THE MARSHY LANDS.)

Mode 3. *b.* (6-note scale.)

SUNG IN THE NURSERY
OF BRACADALE MANSE, SKYE, 1861.

Rather slow.

1. Tha 'n crodh air na lòin, Air na lòin, air na lòin. Tha 'n

Fine.

crodh air na lòin, Is laoigh bheag aig an cas - an.

2. Tha na féidh
   Am Beinn h-Uig [*repeat twice*]
   Tha na féidh
   Am Beinn h-Uig.
   Och! mo dhiùbhail mar thachair.

3. Tha mo shealgair
   'Na shìneadh—[*repeat twice*]
   Tha, etc.
   Na, etc.
   Gun dùil ri tighinn dachaidh.

* 4. 'S è mo Dhonnachadh a bh 'ann,
    'S è mo Dhonnachadh a bh 'ann,
    'S è mo Dhonnachadh a bh 'ann.
    Och! mo dhiùbhail mar thachair!

TRANSLATION (without repetition of phrases).

1. The cattle are on the marshy land, and little calves are following them (at their feet). 2. The deer are in Ben-Uig; and woe's me, what has happened! 3. My huntsman lies prone, with no hope of returning home. 4. My Duncan it was, and woe's me, what has happened!

80.—NA CAORAICH 'S NA GOBHAIR.
(THE SHEEP AND THE GOATS.)

PENTATONIC.

Mode 2.

FROM EIGG.
LEARNT IN EARLY YOUTH IN SKYE.—F. T.

Moderate.

Hi-ù ill o ho! Na caor - aich's na gobh-air. Hi - ù ill o ho! Na

Fine.

gobh-air ri deòl. Ill ò an ill ò! Na gobh-air ri deòl. Ill ò an ill ò! Minn

* This verse is irregular.—F. T.

240

D.C. al Fine.

bheag - a mu 'n chrò. Ill ò an ill ò! Na gobh-air ri deòl. Ill ò an ill ò. Ill

TRANSLATION (without refrains "Hi-ù, etc." and "Ill ò, etc.").

The sheep and the goats; goats suckling their young. Little kids round the fold. Goats, etc.

81.—THA 'N CRODH-LAOIGH 'S AN FHRAOCH.

(THE CALVING-COWS ARE ON THE HEATHER.)

Mode 3 *a.* (6-note scale.)
Moderate.

AN EARLY MEMORY
FROM EIGG, REVIVED, 1861.

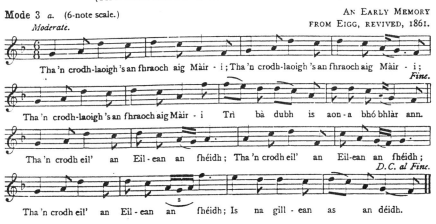

Tha 'n crodh-laoigh 's an fhraoch aig Màir - i ; Tha 'n crodh-laoigh 's an fhraoch aig Màir - i ;

Fine.

Tha 'n crodh-laoigh 's an fhraoch aig Màir - i Trì bà dubh is aon - a bhó bhlàr ann.

Tha 'n crodh eil' an Eil - ean an fhéidh ; Tha 'n crodh eil' an Eil-ean an fhéidh ;

D.C. al Fine.

Tha 'n crodh eil' an Eil - ean an fhéidh ; Is na gill - ean as an déidh.

TRANSLATION.

The calving-cows are on the heather with Mary. Three of them black and one with a white face. The other kine are on Eilean an fhéidh [Island of the Deer], and the lads are following them.

This tune may possibly be connected with the old air "Ca' the yowes."—L. E. B.

82.—CÒ NI BHÙIRICH?

(WHO WILL BELLOW?)

Mode 3. *b.* (6-note scale.)

SUNG IN THE NURSERY
AT BRACADALE MANSE, SKYE, 1861.

Slow.

Fine.

Cò ni bhùir - ich? Ni crodh h-Ùn - ais! Cò ni bhùir - ich?

Ni crodh h-Ùn - ais! Cò ni 'n gé - um - an? Ni crodh Shnì'-e(a)s - ord. *

TRANSLATION.

Who will bellow? The cattle of Hunish. Who will be lowing? The cows of Snizort.

83.—'S TRÀTH CHUIR A GHRIAN.

(EARLY HAS THE SUN.)

Mode 4. *b.* (6-note scale.)

SUNG BY JANET ANDERSON,
(NURSE AT BRACADALE MANSE, SKYE, 1861), WHO LEARNED IT IN EIGG.

Slow.

'S tràth chuir a' ghrian fàilt' air Stroth - o. In - nis a' chruidh-

- laoigh, chaor - ach 's ghobh - ar. Chì mi an òigh, le h-òr - an

fodh - am ; 'sùil air a luaidh, 's a cuach fo chobh - ar.

TRANSLATION.

Early has the sun given greeting to Strotho; pasture of the calving-cows, of sheep, and of goats.
A maiden I behold, singing down yonder; her eye on her loved one, milk-froth on her cogue.†

The old Highland air "Gu ma slàn a chì mi" (see *Songs of the North, Celtic Lyre,* and *Minstrelsy of the Scottish Highlands*) has some likeness to the above tune.— A. G. G.

* Sni'e(a)sord, from Norse *Sneris-fjörðr*; from the personal name Snaerir with 'firth' (fjörðr) added. In place-names in Norway the genitive becomes *Snes.*—G. H.

† Wooden vessel formerly used in the dairy.—F. T. *Cf.* the Lowland-Scottish "cogie."—A. G. G.

84.—CRODH CHAILEIN.
(THE CATTLE OF COLIN.)

Mode 4. *b.* (6-note scale.)

FROM MISS ISABEL CAMERON,
FROM MULL, 1897.

Rather slow.

1. Crodh Chail - ein mo chridh - e, Crodh Chail - ein mo ghaoil; Gu 'n

Fine.

tug - adh crodh Chail - ein, Dhomh bainn' air an fhraoch.

2. Gu 'n tugadh crodh Chailein,
   Dhomh bainn' air an fhraoch,
   Gun chuman, gun bhuarach,
   Gun luaircean, gun laogh.

TRANSLATION.

The cattle of Colin, of Colin beloved; the cattle of Colin give me milk on the heath, without a "cogue"* or a shackle; without a "luaircean"* or calf.

There are various legends relating to the origin of the above song, of which a pleasing version is told by Mr. Neil Macleod, the Bard of Skye. Colin was married to a beautiful young woman, to the chagrin of the fairies, who, casting a spell over her which rendered her invisible, carried her away on the day of her marriage. But she was permitted to return and milk Colin's cows every day, and when she sang to them her sorrowing husband could hear her voice, but never had the consolation of seeing her till a year and a day had expired, when the fairies restored their captive. This song has no refrain. The last two lines of each verse are the first two lines of the next. The "Luaircean" (*see* last verse) was an imitation of a calf placed beside a cow if she had lost her own calf, the skin of which was put on the "Luaircean," the scent from it making her believe that her own offspring was near her; thus soothing the bereaved cow, and inclining her the more readily to yield her milk. The "cogue" was a small wooden milking-vessel, formed of little staves bound about like a tub, with one long stave to form a handle.—F. T.

Other variants, under the title "Colin's Cattle," are in the *Celtic Lyre*, No. 57, *Minstrelsy of the Scottish Highlands, The Thistle, Songs of the North*, etc.; and Captain Fraser quotes "Can you sing balelow?" as a Scottish song to the same tune, thus, probably, identifying it with the "Can ye sew cushions?" of Chambers' *Songs of Scotland prior to Burns.*—A. G. G.

* See notes following.

243

See also a slightly altered harmonised version of Miss Cameron's original air, one of three variants in the *Gesto Coll.* The air here given has a strong likeness to that of the favourite ballad "Donald's Return to Glencoe" (*see* "Glencoe," *Complete Petrie Coll.* and *Journal*, vol. ii. No. 8, p. 171, for traditional examples). I have noted a variant, to "The Pride of Glencoe." in County Waterford. For a Perthshire setting, *see* the *Killin Coll.* edited by Charles Stewart (Edinburgh: Maclachlan & Stewart).— L. E. B.

GROUP III.—ANCIENT HEROIC LAYS.

85.—LAOIDH DHIARMAD.

(THE LAY OF DIARMID.)

Mode 2. *a.* (6-note scale.)

SUNG BY MARGARET MACLEOD (COTTAR),
PORTREE, SKYE, 1870.

Rather slow.

1.·'S ann   an raoir   bu ghorm   an tul - ach, Gè dearg   an diu   e   le   fuil Dhiar-mad ;

Fine.

'S gur b-ann leis   an Fheinn   bu duil - ich.   Mur   a   bith - eadh Fionn   'ga iarr - aidh.

2. "Fhinn, nach toir thu dhomh-sa deoch,
   Dhearbh mhic a righ is mo chobhair,
   Tighearn mo bhiadh, agus m'aodaich?"
   "Och-òin-a-rì! 's mi nach tabhair!

3. Cha toir mise dhuit-sa deoch,
   Ni mò a chaisgeas mi t'iotadh,
   'S beag a rinn thu riamh dha m'leas,
   Is mór a rinn thu dha m'aimhleas."

   Canar gun fhonn:
   An sin bhàsaich Diarmaid air an tom.

TRANSLATION.

1. Green last night was the knoll, though it be red to-day with the blood of Diarmid ; and grievous were this to the Feinn, had it not been the desire of Fionn. 2. (*Diarmid*) "Fionn, wilt thou not give me to drink, thou true son of a king, and my succour ; lord over my food and my clothing?" (*Fionn*) "Och oin-a-ree! that will not I! 3. I will not give a drink to thee, and neither shall I quench thy thirst ; help thou didst never offer me, nor didst render but to my ruin." (Spoken) Then died Diarmid upon the knoll.

The above tune was contributed by me to the *Gesto Coll.* (App. p. 12) without words. For other versions of the story and words, see *Waifs and Strays of Celtic Tradition*, vol. iv. p. 52 ; J. F. Campbell's *West Highland Tales*, vol. iii. p. 50 ; *Leabhar na Fèinne*, p. 151 ; and *Gillies' Coll.* (1786), p. 284.—F. T.

Cf. the air "The Lay of Diarmid" in Thomas Pattison's *Twelve Gaelic Songs.* The Gaelic song which he prints is, however, in a different metre, and tells the story of Diarmid's fight with the boar, ending with his victory over it. There are eight

245

verses, but it is possible that these do not include the whole of the song. *See*, too, another "Lay of Diarmid"—also from Skye—in Mrs. Kennedy Fraser's *Songs of the Hebrides*. This is the lament of Grainne over her hero, both tune and words being different from the above.—A. G. G.

86.—LAOIDH FHRAOICH.

(THE LAY OF FRAOCH.)

Mode 1. *a. b.* (7-note scale.)

SUNG BY MARGARET MACLEOD (COTTAR), PORTREE, SKYE, 1870.

Grave.

1. Thàin - ig ea - slaint - e throm, throm, Air nigh - ean [?] nan corn fial, Ag - us chuir i fios gu Fraoch, 'S dh 'fhid-ir an laoch ciod è a miann. 2. Thubh - airt i nach biodh i slàn, Mur faigh 'dh i làn a bas mhaoth, De chaorr - ann an lod - ain f huair, O 's gun a bhith 'g am buain ach Fraoch.

Fine.

3. "Cnuasach sud nach d 'rinn mi riamh,"
   Arsa Fionn mac-Idhaidh nan arm geur,
   "'S ged nach d 'rinn mi 'n cnuasach s 'riamh,
   Thèid mise bhuain chaorann do Mhaidhbh."

4. Dh 'fhalbh è, 's cha b 'è turus àigh ;
   Shnàmh è gu grinn air an loch,
   Is fhuair è bhéist na sior-throm suain,
   'S a craos suas ris an dos.

TRANSLATION.

1. There came an overpowering illness to the daughter of [* ?] of the generous drinking-horns, who sent a message to Fraoch, and the hero asked what was her desire. 2. She declared that she would never be well unless she were to receive the full of her tender palms of rowan-berries from the little cold pool (or lake), but that no other was to pluck them than Fraoch. 3. "A fruit-gathering like that have I never done," said Fraoch Mac Idhaidh (son of Idad) of keen-edged weapons, "and though I have never done the same, I will go and gather the rowan-berries for Maive." 4. He went on his unpropitious way, and gracefully he swam the loch, and found the monster fast asleep, with her great mouth up near the cluster of fruit.

For other versions of this lay, see *Leabhar na Feinne*, p. 29 ; *Gillies' Coll.* (1786), p. 107 ; J. F. Campbell's *West Highland Tales*, vol. iv. p. 78. The air was contributed

* Name forgotten here. It was no doubt some form of "Eochaidh," the sick woman's father.

by me to the *Gesto Coll.* (App. p. 12) without words. For a rendering of the complete Lay of Fraoch, with the older account and relative literature, see *The Geste of Fraoch and the Dragon*, by George Henderson (Edinburgh: John Grant, George IV. Bridge. 1910).—F. T.

"The Lay of Fraoch" seems more of the nature of a recitative or chant than a tune, and probably forms a typical instance of the kind of music to which the most ancient Celtic ballads were sung. The tune has here been assigned to Mode 1, but it is questionable whether it does not really belong to Mode 3, with the ♭7th. The peculiarly flat effect of the G♮ in this tune suggests a modified interval, and in other tunes in this collection where a similar *extra*-flat note occurs, this note seems to me to correspond to the occasionally flattened E of Modes 1, 2, and 3, as suggested in my schedule.—A. G. G.

Like a tune in *Journal*, vol. i. p. 15, No. 2, this air is in a mode showing Mixolydian compass and Dorian influence. *Cf.* the introductory phrases of both tunes.—J. A. F. M.

The opening phrase, used also in "Macrimmon's Lament," is exceedingly characteristic of the West Highlands.—L. E. B.

In *The Death of Fraoch*, a version published for J. MacCormick and W. Muir (Ritchie, Iona, 1887), and now out of print, there is an air given which was current in Mull. The old lay has seven syllables in each line. As noted from the singing of Mr. MacCormick, the air is as follows in sol-fa:

KEY F sharp.

s	:— .l	s	:ɴ	d	:— .ɴ	s	:—
s	:— .l	s	:ɴ	r	:— .r	ɴ	:—
s	:— .s	s	:— .l	s	:— .ɴ	s	:—
l	:— .l	s	:ɴ	r	:— .r	d	: *Fine.*
d	:— .d	d	:r	d	:— .d	d	:—
r	:— .d	d	:— .t₁	l₁	:— .s₁	s₁	:—
d	:— .d	d	:r	d	:— .l₁	d	:—
r	:— .r	r	:d	r	:— .ɴ	r	:—

—G. H.

247

87.—LAOIDH OSCAIR.

(THE LAY OF OSCAR.)

PENTATONIC.
Mode 4.

SUNG BY MARGARET MACLEOD (COTTAR),
PORTREE, SKYE, 1870.

1.(*Oisean.*) "Sin 'nuair chunn - a mis - e Fionn ; Air an tul - aich os mo chionn ;
Fine.

Sil - eadh fal - a air a rosg ; 'S thionnd-aich Fionn a chùl - thaobh rium - sa."

2. (*Fionn.*) "Mo Ghaol fhéin thu! Laogh mo laoigh thu ;
Leanabh mo leinibh ghil chaoimh thu ;
Mo chridhe leum dhuit mar lon ;
'S mo chreach léir! Cha 'n éirich Oscar!"

TRANSLATION.

1. (*Ossian*) "It was then that I saw Fionn, on the hillock up above, from his eyelids shedding blood; then on me his back he turned." 2. (*Fionn*) "My own love, thou! Calf of my calf! * Child of my fair, gentle child. My heart leaps to thee like an elk. Oscar, alas, will rise no more."

The air of this lay, without words, was contributed by me to the *Gesto Coll.* (App. p. 12). For versions of the lay, see *Waifs and Strays of Celtic Tradition,* vol. iv. p. 29; J. F. Campbell's *West Highland Tales,* vol. iii. p. 305 (64 verses); *Leabhar na Féinne,* pp. 184-195 ; and *Gillies' Coll.* (1786), p. 313.—F. T.

"Thionndaich" is a dialectal variant for "thionndaidh."—G. H.

88.—CUMHA DHIARMAD.

(LAMENT FOR DIARMID.)

Mode 3. *a* [with ♭7th]. (6-note scale.)
MIXOLYDIAN INFLUENCE.

SUNG BY MRS. M'VICAR (SPINNER),
NORTH UIST, 1871.

†(*a*) Bheir mi o hó rionn o hó. (*b*) Tha tùch - ar - an beag air m 'an - ail.

(*c*) Bheir mi o hó rionn o hó. (*d*) Ag - us crith-each 'na mo chliabh. (*e*) Bheir mi hó rionn o hó !

* *i.e.* "My fondest dear one."

248

(Ch.)   *D.C. al Fine.*

(*f*) E-ho ì   ri   ri - ibh - ag   o   ho. (*g*) Hó   rionn o   ho,   ho   ro.

†In this song the lines marked (*b*) and (*d*) form the verse couplet. The other lines are refrain and are repeated with every verse. The refrain simply conveys the idea of: " My croon will be o hó rionn o hó," with variations of the vowel sounds to suit the music. The Solo Singer *opens* the song with bar 1, and Chorus repeats it.

TRANSLATION (without refrains).

1. "There is oppression on my breathing, and trembling in my breast. 2. May *Brian remove the hoarseness ere my beloved hear my voice! 3. I heed not the return of day; I care not though the sun has gone down; 4. and vain is everything on earth, since fellowship with thee is gone. 5. No more do lovers raise their eye since on thy cheek the earth has been laid. 6. Yellow were thy locks, ruddy was thy cheek, and beautiful thy countenance. 7. With thee would I roam from north to south, and from south to north with thee would I go. 8. Beauteous Diarmid! thy 'beauty-spot' laid hold on me, and I am wounded entirely. 9. Since yesterday hast thou wounded me, thy like was not in the Féinn." (*Fionn*) " Diarmid, wilt thou not measure the boar? How many feet from his snout to his tail?... Then, when thou didst measure the boar, thou didst receive the wound in thy heel, and following that, thy death." [By one of Diarmid's followers.]

This song, believed to have been composed by one of the devoted followers of Diarmid, was only imperfectly remembered by a few elderly women thirty-eight years ago. For versions of words and story, see *Waifs and Strays of Celtic Tradition* (Lord A. Campbell), vol. iv. p. 52; *West Highland Tales* (J. F. Campbell of Islay), vol. iii. p. 50; *Leabhar na Féinne*, p. 151. I contributed the tune of the above lament, with the Gaelic words, to the *Gesto Coll.* (App. p. 26).—F. T.

This tune is Mixolydian, and a variant of "Comhairl' Oisein" (No. 89).—J. A. F. M.

89.—COMHAIRL' OISEIN DHA 'MHÀTHAIR.

(OSSIAN'S WARNING TO HIS MOTHER.)

Mode 3 [with ♭7th].   SUNG BY MARGARET MACLEOD (COTTAR),
MIXOLYDIAN INFLUENCE.   PORTREE, SKYE, 1871, AND MRS. M'VICAR, N. UIST, 1871.
Slow.

(S.) V.   R.

1. †(*a*) Ma's   tu   mo   mhàth-air 's   gur   fiadh   thu.   (*b*) Bheir   mi   hó   rionn

* One of the gods of Celtic heathendom. His name occurs in Scott's "Lady of the Lake." He, with Iuchar and Iucharba, formed the old triad of Gadelic myth.—G. H.

249

(f) O   hi o ho, hó ·   ro. (g) Bheir mi o hó rionn o   ho.

† The lines marked (a) and (c) form the verse couplets in this song. The other lines are refrain and are repeated with every verse.

TRANSLATION.

1. If thou be my mother, who art a deer,* be up before the rising of the sun. 2. Go over the hill ere heat come on, and beware of the action of dogs. 3. If thou go upon the mountains high, beware of the clan of the "cairds," the sons of the artificers and their dogs. 4. Two dogs and ten on a leash they have, and his own dog in each man's hand. 5. If thou reach the low glens, guard thee against the forest clan, the sons of the forest and their dogs. 6. Two dogs and ten on a leash they have, and his own dog in each man's hand. 7. If thou go into the deep glens, beware of the children of the smith.

When written down by me, in 1871, this song was almost forgotten among the old folk in Skye, but both there and in the Long Island the tradition lingers that Ossian's mother was a deer. For story and words, see *Waifs and Strays of Celtic Tradition* (Lord A. Campbell), vol. iv. p. 79, and *Leabhar na Féinne*, p. 198. The air to the above, with the Gaelic words, was contributed by me to the *Gesto Coll.* (App. p. 21).—F. T.

This tune is pentatonic in framework, but one flat 7th occurs.—A. G. G.

* The deer-parentage of Ossian (Gaelic "Oisian," Irish "Oisín," both with short *o*) is referred to in the *Book of Leinster* (12th century). The name is a diminutive from G. *os*, Early Irish *oss* = a deer, elk ; the proto-Celtic being *ukso-*, and cognate in root with English *ox* ; Sanscrit *ukshán*, a bull. Similar old Gaelic formations are Os-bran, Os-chú, Os-fer, Os-gen. The name is indubitably of Celtic origin (*v.* Kuno Meyer's *Fianaighecht* : Royal Irish Academy, 1910). It is probable that "Oscar" means ultimately "deer-lover, deer-friend," the root *os*, *oss*, pointing to the animal-parentage of the legend being retained in the name.—G. H.

90.—AM BRÒN BINN,—AISLING RIGH BHREATAINN.

(THE MELODIOUS SORROW,—THE DREAM OF THE KING OF BRITAIN.)

Mode 4. *b.* (6-noté scale.)
Rather slow.

SUNG BY MARGARET MACLEOD (COTTAR),
PORTREE, ISLE OF SKYE, 1870.

*(a) Hó ró hùg o hug o. (b) 1. Chunn-aic Righ Bhreat-ainn na shuain. (c) Thug - aibh i ó,

Sìnt thug - aibh i. (d) 'N aon - a bhean as àill - e snuadh fo 'n ghréin.

2. Gu'm b'fhearr leis tuiteam 'na gean
   Na comhradh fhear mar è fhéin

3. Labhair Fios-falaich gu fial :
   Théid mi fhéin 'ga h-iarraidh dhuit,

4. Mi fhéin, mo ghille 's mo chù.
   'N ar triùir a shireadh na mnài.

(*Fios-falaich*)

5. "'S ann agam fhéin a ta an long
   As luaith a chuireas tonn 'na déidh ;

6. 'S ann agam fhéin a ta an cù
   As luaith' a chuireas sùil ri seilg."

. . . . .

7. "Fad sheachd seachdanan 's dà mhios,
   Bha sinn sgìth ri siubhail cuain

8. Mu'm facas cala no fonn
   Far am faodadh an long tàmh."

. . . . .

9. "Mach gu iomall a' chuain ghairbh,
   Chunnacas caisteal, mìn-gheal gorm ;

10. 'S an àm dhomh tèarnadh ri bhun,
    Thàinig slabhruidh dhubh a nuas.

11. Cha do ghabh mi eagal no fiamh
    'S chaidh mi fhéin 'nam ruith suas.

12. Chunnacas a Bhean bhréid-gheal òg,
    Anns a' chathair òir a stigh,

13. Brat shìoda fo dà bhonn
    Bu lion-mhór ann cuach, le còrn.

(*Fios-falaich*)

14. "An t-aobhar mu'n d'thàinig mi steach
    Nì mi è mu'n téid mi mach.

15. Suidhidh sinn, 's traoghamaid feirg
    'S cuiridh sinn cealg mu'n Fhear mhór."

(*A'bhain-tighearn*)

16. "Trobhad 's cuir do cheann air mo ghlùn,
    'S gu'n seinninn dhuit cèol is cruit ;"

17. Cruit an làimh na Finne-gheal ùr,
    As guirme sùil, 's as gile déud.

. . . . .

18. Thuit esan na shìor-throm suain
    An déis bhi cuartachadh cuain ghairbh ;

19. Thug i'n claidheamh nios bho chrios
    'S dh'fhàg i è gun fhios da marbh.

20. Sin agaibh deireadh mo sgeòil,
    Mar a sheinneadh am Bròn Bìnn.

*In the above song the lines of the stanzas are introduced in each round of the lay to correspond with positions (*b*) and (*d*).

(*Refrain*: Hó ró, etc.) 1. The King of Britain beheld, in his deep slumber, (*Ch.* : Thugaibh i, etc.) the one woman of most lovely aspect beneath the sun. (R.) 2. He would rather find favour with her, than have converse with another like himself. 3. Said Fios-falaich with right good-will : "I shall go in search of her ; 4. myself, my gillie, and my dog ; the three of us the woman to find." 5. (*Fios-falaich* speaks) "'Tis I myself possess a vessel, the most swift to leave a wave behind ; 6. 'tis I also own a dog, to the chase most quick to set his eye." . . . 7. "During seven weeks and two months, we were weary traversing seas, 8. ere we saw a harbour, or land where the vessel might find repose. 9. Out on the border of the wild sea a castle I beheld of smooth white stone, on verdant ground ; 10. and when I drew near the base, a black chain was coming down, 11. causing me no fear nor dread ; and running I went up. 12. A white-coifed young woman then I saw, sitting on a chair of gold, 13. a cloth of silk beneath her feet, and numerous, there, were cups and horns." 14. (*Fios-falaich* speaks) "The purpose for which I came in, I shall perform, ere I go out : 15. seating ourselves, abating wrath, the Big Man let us then beguile." 16. (*Lady* speaks) "Come lay thy head upon my knee, that I may sing to thee with harp." 17. Harp in the hand of the maiden, fair and young, of eye the most blue, and whitest teeth. . . . 18. Then fell he fast asleep after crossing stormy seas. 19. Down from his girdle taking the sword, unknown to himself, she left him dead. 20. Thus have ye the end of my tale : how the Melodious Sorrow used to be sung.

Cf. *Leabhar na Féinne*, p. 208. "Righ Breatainn."—F. T.

This lay, identified by Dr. Henderson as a version of one of the Sir Gawain stories, also recalls in its opening incidents the Welsh romance (in the *Mabinogion*) of "The Dream of Maxen Wledig," the British-born Emperor of Rome—identified with the Emperor Maximus, who was overthrown at Aquileia, A.D. 388. In this Welsh mediæval romance, as in the "Dream of the King of Britain," the royal dreamer sends emissaries over land and sea in search of the beautiful maiden of his dream. The "black 'chain coming down" seems to refer to the lowered draw-bridge of the castle in which she dwelt ; similarly in the story of Maxen Wledig, on the arrival of his messengers in the island of Britain "the gate of the castle was open" and they went in and found the maiden "sitting on a chair of ruddy gold," and surrounded by all the details of magnificence which the Emperor had seen in his dream. So far the resemblance is close, but the sequel of the Maxen Wledig story is different, there being no strife with Helen's kindred. This motif of a dream about a beautiful maiden and the subsequent search for her is also found in English folk-song. See "The Cornish Young Man" (*Journal*, vol. ii. p. 53) and "The Knight's Dream" (*Journal*, vol. ii. p. 273), which seem to be degraded relics of this old story, retaining, however, a suggestion of the Celtic nationality of the hero—described as "Cornish" or "outlandish" by the Saxon narrator—just as the "outlandish knight from the north lands" of other English ballads suggests the Norse origin of his malevolent prototype as found in Scandinavian ballads.—A. G. G.

I have noted a very similar air to this (a variant of No. 91, "Hó ró hùg-o")

from the singing of a very old crofter at Cross in the Arisaig district of Inverness-
shire, to words describing the departure of a soldier, a beautiful man, to the wars.
—L. E. B.

In this variant there is a gap between vv. 15 and 16. In a version I have, the
lady here says:

> " Gallant! the main thou hast traversed;
> for thy kindly greeting woe's me:
> The Lord of this Castle he recks not
> of thy valour or frailty."

Then Fios-falaich, properly Sir Gauvain, speaks:

> " An it please thee, kindly lady,
> his love or his hate liketh me."

Some lines are again lacking, but the lay proceeds:

> " In hiding she placed Sir Gauvain.
> Then entered the Castle's great lord."

It is to the castle's great lord, the Fear Mór, that stanza 16 is addressed, and it is
he who is beheaded. Fios-falaich is a folk-corruption for Sir Bhalbhuaidh, Sir
Ghalmhai, Sir Galahad (Welsh Gwalchmai). It is the "wife and nephew incident,"
and the King of Britain is King Arthur. For fuller discussion of this lay, *see* my
version, with translation, in the *Festschrift* to Professor Kuno Meyer (Niemeyer, Halle
on the Saale).—G. H.

91.—HÓ RÓ, HÙG O, HÚG O.

Mode 3-4. *b. See Note.* (6-note scale.)   SUNG BY MARGARET GILLIES (COTTAR),
Rather slow.   BRACADALE, SKYE, 1862.

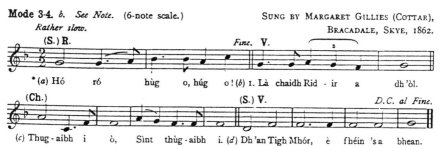

* In this song the lines of the stanzas are introduced in each round to correspond with positions (*b*) and (*d*).

(*Refrain*: Hó ró, etc.)   1. On a day, a knight (*Ch.* : Thugaibh, etc.) and his wife went to the Great House to drink. (R.)   2. When he was carving, he cut his finger, and injured the flesh to the grey bone. 3. From the fear he felt about his finger, the breath went from him in vapour.   4. His friends gathered round to bear him to his grave without delay.   5. His wife gave utterance to great oaths that she would not move from the tombstone,   6. till she should be laid beneath the sod, herself and her spouse.

The above tune with Gaelic words, was contributed by me to the *Gesto Coll.* (App. p. 15).   Several narrative songs, such as " The Melodious Sorrow, or Dream of the King of Britain," and " The Lay of the Black Dog " (see *Leabhar na Féinne*, pp. 91, 208), were sung to the same air with similar refrain.—F. T.

Another repeating tune, in which it is difficult to fix on any note as the " end."—A. G. G.

GROUP IV.—SONGS TO CHIEFS AND OTHERS.

92.—FEAR BHÀLAI.

(MACDONALD OF VĀLEY.)

Mode 3. *a.* (6-note scale.)
Moderate.

Sung by Harriet M'Vicar (Spinner),
North Uist, 1870.

(S.) V.   **R.**

1. 'N raoir chunn - a mi'n ais - ling. O hi ri ri ò.

(Ch.)   *Fine.*

Chall éil - e, ho ro, o hi ri ri ò.

TRANSLATION (without refrains and ch.).

1. Last night I saw in my dream, 2. which on awaking did not prove true, 3. that thou, dearest, hadst come home. 4. Grandson of Sir James* of the banners, 5. successful is it thy wont to be on the foray. 6. With thee, the horsemen would rise ; 7. in thy company, wine, abundant as showers, would be taken. 8. O King of Heaven ! Let not the breeze be strong ! 9. Keep the wind peaceful and subdued, 10. so that the warriors may return !

[By his foster-mother, 17th century.]

I contributed the above tune, with the Gaelic words, to the *Gesto Coll.* (App. p. 22).—F. T.

93.—ORAN DO MHAC-IAIN-'IC-SHEUMAIS.

(A SONG TO THE SON OF JOHN-SON-OF-JAMES.)

Mode 3. *b.* (6-note scale.)
Slow.

Sung by Harriet M'Vicar (Spinner),
North Uist, 1870.

(S.)

1. A Mhic - Iain - 'ic - Sheum - ais, Tha do sgeul air m'air - e.

* Sir James Macdonald of Sleat joined the Marquis of Montrose in 1645.

R. .... V.

Air fair a lail ó,   Air fair a lail ó! Bho'n là thug thu'n cuan d'i Bha

(Ch.)

gruaim air na beann - aibh. Hi   ó.   Hi ri rith - ibh ò   hi eil - e.   Hi

Fine.

ó,   Hi rith-ibh ò   rò   ao   ò! Chall eil - ibh hò ró, Hao ri o   ho i   ò.

2.   *Solo*: *Bho'n là thug thu'n cuan d'i,
     Bha gruaim air na beannaibh,
   Refrain: Air faire lail ó, air faire lail ó.
     Bha smal air na speuran
     'S bha na reultan 'gam falach.
      Chorus: Hi ó, hi-ri, etc.
3.   'S è Mac-Iain-'ic-Sheumais
     Duine treubhach smiorail.
4.   Gruaidh ruiteach na féile
     Mar éibhleag 'ga garadh.
5.   Bu cheannard roimh shluagh thu
     Dol suas troimh thir ain-iùil.

6.   Le claidheamh geur cruadhach,
     'S dé ! cha d'fhuaireadh sgann' air.
7.   Cha'n iarradh tu cluasag
     Ach cluain am bi gaineamh.
8.   Nam biodh agam curach,
     Gu'n cuirinn air chuan i,
9.   Is gille maith turuis
     Bhitheadh furachail uaithe,
10.   Feuch am faighinn naigheachd,
     Air mac an duin 'uasail.

[Le Mhuime.]

* Two couplets are sung as a verse, the last couplet of one verse forming the first couplet of the next.

TRANSLATION.

1. O thou son of John-son-of-James, for tidings of thee I am waiting. (*Ref.* : Air, etc.) Since the day on which thou didst turn thy galley towards the open sea, the mountains have been in gloom, (*Ch.* : Hi, etc.) 2. darkness has overspread the skies, and the stars have been hiding. 3. John's son, the son of James, is a valorous and vigorous man ; 4. ruddy, of the generous countenance, like an ember enkindling. 5. Going through a strange land, a true leader of men art thou, 6. with a sharp sword of steel, in which most certainly no fault might be found. 7. No pillow wouldst thou desire but a meadow, where there should be sand. 8. If I had a skiff I should launch her on the sea, 9. with an excellent emissary who should look well around him, 10. so that I might gain tidings of the son of him who was of good descent.

[By his foster-mother.]

Donald Macdonald, the renowned son of John, son of James, was reputed to be in every respect, for bravery and sound judgment, the most able warrior that had ever been in Clan Donald. When, about the year 1601, Donald Glas Macleod from Harris was on a foray in North Uist and Benbecula, John's-son-the-son-of-James heard the lamentations of his foster-mother at Iomar-fad, on beholding her only cow being driven away by the marauders. Hastening to the rescue, he defeated them, slew Donald Glas, and restored the cow to his foster-mother. He buried the head of Donald Glas in a knoll at

Càrinish in North Uist, where the ruins are still standing of a church built prior to the Reformation. But Macdonald was himself grievously wounded in the fray, having been pierced by twelve arrows in his back and limbs. When the arrows were being extracted and his wounds dressed, his foster-mother set women to waulk a web of cloth, and to sing loudly the above song which she had once composed in her nursling's praise so that his groans might not be heard by his followers. Donald Gorm, the Chief, gave to the Son of John-the-son-of-James lands in Trotternish in Skye, in consideration of his great merit. One of his descendants was Alan Macdonald of Kingsburgh, the husband of Flora Macdonald. *Cf.* a version of words in Sinclair's *An t-Oranaiche*, p. 131. My air to another version of Gaelic words is in *Gesto Coll.* (App. p. 58).—F. T.

94.—ALASDAIR 'MHIC, O-HO.

(ALEXANDER, SON OF COLKITTO.)

Mode 2. *a. b.** (7-note scale.)
Moderate, loud.

SUNG BY MRS. MACLEAN (WIFE OF CROFTER), CASTLEBAY, BARRA, 1902.

(S.)

1. Al-as-dair mhic, O - hó! Choll-aghasd-a, O - hó   As do làimh-s gu'n, O - hó,

R.   (Ch.)

Earb-ainn tap-adh, trom   eil-e. † Ohall eil - ibh o - hì,   Ohall o ho ro, Ohall eil - ibh o - hao, Ohall o ho ro.

Chall - ail - o, hao - ri   o, Chall · o ho ro, Hao i o   hó, trom   eil - e.

2. ‡As do làimh gu'n, o-hó!
   Earbainn tapadh, o-hó!
   Mharbhadh Tighearn, o-hó!
   Ach-nam-breac leat, trom eile.

   Chorus: Chall eilibh, etc.

3. Thiodhlaiceadh an
   Oir an loch è

4. 'S ged 's beag mi fhéin.
   Bhuail mi ploc air.

5. Chuala mi'n dé
   Sgeul nach b'ait leam.

6. Glascho a bhith
   Dol 'na lasair,

7. 'S Obar-re'oin (Obar-Dhe'oin)
   'N déidh chreachadh.

* B has been taken as the tonic of this tune.—A. G. G.

† "Trom" meaning "heavy," or "melancholy:" if for "Chall" we read "Call," the chorus might be interpreted "Another loss, ohí! another loss, ohó! etc. (other) heavy (loss or woe)!"—G. H.

‡ The last couplet of each stanza is repeated as the first couplet of the next.

257

1. Alexander, thou son of excellent Coll, from thy hand I should expect deeds of valour.
(*Ref.* : Trom eile. *Ch.* : Chall, etc.) 2. The Laird of Achnabreck was slain by thee, 3. and buried near the loch. 4. And small though I myself may be, even I did cast a clod on him. 5. I heard tidings yesterday that did not cause me any joy: 6. that the City of Glasgow was in flames, 7. and Aberdeen being despoiled.

Alexander Macdonald, son of Colkitto, was a renowned general in the army of the Marquis of Montrose in 1644.—F. T.

95.—ORAN DO GHILLEASBUIG OG, A HEISGEIR.
(SONG TO YOUNG GILLEASBUIG OF HEISKIR.)

PENTATONIC.
Modes 3 and 4.
Rather slow.

SUNG BY MARY ROSS,
FROM KILLMALUAG, SKYE, 1897.

Ho - ro o hùg hoir-ionn ò. Fall-ain gu 'n till thu ! Ho ró o - hùg, hoir-ionn ò.

1. Gur h-è mis - e tha fo mhul - ad An tìr - a-mhur - ain, 's an t-siob-ainn.

2. Dalta-cìche mo mhàthar,
   Is càch ag ràdh nach till thu !

3. Ghilleasbuig òig a H-eisgeir,
   Bu tu aoibhneas nan nigh 'neag.

4. Mo cheisd, fear a chùil bhuidhe
   Ni a bhruthach a dhìreadh ;

5. Mo ghaol, fear a chùil dualaich,
   'S nan cuaileanan rìomhach,

6. Bu tu sgiobair na fairge
   Ri là gailbheach 's droch shìde.

7. 'S è do thurus 'Ghilleasbuig
   Thug leagadh do m 'inntinn :

8. Tha do thighean 'g an rùsgadh
   Sgeula thùrsach ra innseadh ;

9. Do chuid eòrn' air an achadh,
   'S gu 'n téid pailteas a dhìth dheth ;

10. Do chuid mòine gun chruachadh,
    Sgeula chruaidh leam ri chluinntinn ;

11. Tha do "cheilp" air na clachan,
    'S cha 'n fhaic Sasunn a chaoidh e.
    [A chomhdhalta.]

(*Solo Ref. and Ch.* : Ho, ro, o hùg, hoirionn ò, Safely do thou return, Ho, ro, etc.) 1. How mournful am I, in the land of sea-bent and of sand-drift ! (S.R. and Ch.) 2. Thou nursling of my mother, they say that thou wilt not return. 3. Young Gilleasbuig of Heiskir, the delight art thou of the maidens. 4. My beloved is he of the yellow hair, who actively climbs the steep hill-side. 5. My love is he of the curling locks and the beautiful ringlets; 6. a bold sailor at sea on a day of tempest and wild weather.... 7. It is thy journey, O Gilleasbuig, which has been the cause of my sorrow. 8. Thy houses are being laid low—a tale grievous to relate; 9. thy barley is lying on the field, and much of it will spoil; 10. thy peats have not been put in the stack—tidings painful for me to hear; 11. thy kelp is still upon the stones, and in England will never be seen.

[By his foster-sister.]

This song was composed in the eighteenth century. The name "Gilleasbuig," literally "the gillie, or lad, of the bishop," is represented in English by "Archibald." —F. T.

96.—ORAN IONNDRAINN (i.).

(A SONG OF LONGING REMEMBRANCE.)

SUNG BY MR. MACLACHAN, DERVAIG, ISLAND OF MULL, 1901. HEARD ALSO AT QUINISH, I. OF MULL.

PENTATONIC.
Mode 4. *
Moderate.

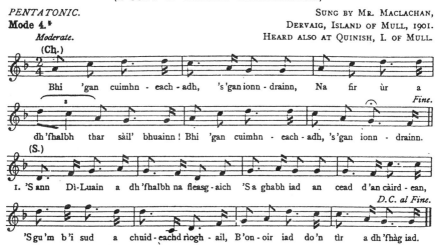

Bhi 'gan cuimhn - each - adh, 's 'gan ionn - drainn, Na fir ùr a *Fine.*

dh'fhalbh thar sàil' bhuainn! Bhi 'gan cuimhn - each - adh, 's 'gan ionn - drainn.

1. 'S ann Dì-Luain a dh'fhalbh na fleasg - aich 'S a ghabh iad an cead d'an càird - ean, *D.C. al Fine.*

'S gu'm b'i sud a chuid - eachd rìogh - ail, B'on - oir iad do'n tìr a dh'fhàg iad.

96.—ORAN IONNDRAINN (ii.).

(A SONG OF LONGING REMEMBRANCE.)

Mode 5. *a.* (6-note scale.)
Moderate.

SUNG BY MARY ROSS, FROM KILLMALUAG, SKYE, 1901.

Bhi 'g an cuimhn each - adh 's 'gan ionndr - ainn

* G has been taken as the tonic of this tune.—A. G. G.

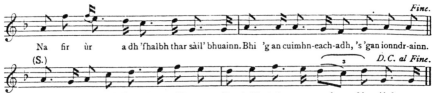

Na   fir   ùr   a dh 'fhalbh thar sàil' bhuainn. Bhi 'g an cuimhn-each-adh, 's 'gan ionndr-ainn.

(S.)   D.C. al Fine.

1. 'S ann Dì-Luain a dh 'fhalbh na gill - ean,   'S a ghabh iad   an cead   d 'an càird - ean.

2. * Caiptin Donnachadh, mac Mhic-Dhùghaill,
   Leis an d 'fhalbh na fiùrain àluinn.

3. 'S na 'm bu mhac thu mar an t-athair
   Dheanadh tu 'n toirt dhachaidh sàbhailt.

4. Theid iad uile deas' n an tarruing
   Grad mar dhealanach· gu làmhach.

5. 'S geal an claidheamh 's an crios-guaille,
   Gu 'n éireadh buaidh le sluagh mo, ghràidh-sa.

6. 'S ann ·Dì-Luain a dh 'fhalbh na gillean
   'S leam bu mhilis an deoch slàinte.

* In Version i. the last couplet of each verse is repeated as the first of the next.

TRANSLATION.

(*Chorus* : Remembering and longing for them, the gallant men who went from us over the sea. Remembering, etc.) 1. It was on Monday they departed, after taking leave of their friends ; a company of royal aspect, and an honour to the country which they had left. (Ch.) 2. With Captain Duncan of Clan-Dougall the handsome young men went away. 3. If thou be a son like his father, thou wilt lead them safely home again ! 4. In good order they will advance, swift as lightning to fire. 5. Bright their swords and shoulder-belts. May victory be with them whom I love. 6. On Monday the lads set out, and pleasant to me was the farewell drinking to their health.

Version i. was popular in Mull and Argyll about a century ago, when, under the command of Captain Duncan Macdougall of Dunollie, a company of Argyll men went to Ireland to maintain order during a period of general disquiet. A song with similar refrain, but to a different tune (Version ii.), was current in Skye at the same time, and was revived and crooned by some of the old folk when there was a renewal of emigration to the Colonies in 1860.—F. T.

The mode of the first melody, taking G to be the tonic, illustrates the fourth position of the Scottish pentatonic scale, as numbered in my preface. Dr. Culwick quotes "Tiernna Mayo" as an Irish example of this mode, without 3rd or 6th degree. "Blythe, blythe and merry was she" is given as a Scottish example of the same mode in Helmholtz's *Sensations of Tone* (translated by A. J. Ellis). The latter tune is identified by Captain Fraser as a Gaelic air : "An gunna cutach " (= "The cutty gun ").—A. G. G.

97.—ORAN DO MHAC-GRIOGAIR O RUADH-SHRUTH.

(A SONG TO MACGREGOR OF RUARO.)

PENTATONIC.
Modes 3 and 1.

Sung by Janet Anderson (Nurse),
Bracadale Manse, Skye, 1861.

Moderately slow.

1. Tha mul-ad, tha mul-ad, Tha mul-ad 'g am lion-adh; Tha mul-ad bochd truagh orm, Nach dual domh chaoidh dìr-eadh. 2. Tha mul-ad bochd truagh orm, Nach dual domb chaoidh dìr-eadh, Mu Mhac-Griog-air a Ruadh-shruth, Dh'am bu dual bhi 'n Gleann Lio' - ann.

TRANSLATION.

1. Sorrow, deep sorrow has seized me; a despairing grief which I am not destined to overcome; 2. for the sake of MacGregor of Ruaro, whose birthright is Glenlyon—3. MacGregor of the banners, in whose praise loudly the bag-pipes used to resound; 4. whose badge was the pine ascending the mountain-side.... 8. Though a rude fellow were to smite me, I would not complain; 9. though an injury were done to me, O Thou! [Lord!] Who would avenge it 10. while those who would take my part are in the burying-ground, down yonder? 11. Those who would stand for my rights, sorely do I miss! 15. This advice I would fain give thee, if thou wouldst accept it: 16. when thou goest to the inn, take but one drink, 17. and take thy dram standing; and provide well for thy men; 18. be not too particular about the vessel, but use the ladle or baler; 19. let the autumn be to thee as winter, and the summer as early spring; 20. make thy bed among the rocks, and sleep but lightly. 21. Though the squirrel be rare, there is a way to find her; 22. and proud though the falcon be, she may be taken with guile.

[By his foster-mother.]

This MacGregor of Ruaro was executed with other outlaws in Edinburgh, in the year 1604. The burden of the song is the advice given him by his foster-mother to ensure his safety against the observation of vigilant and numerous enemies. There is no refrain, but, instead, the two last lines of every verse become the two first lines of the verse following, and may be sung as a chorus. The above English verses are translations of the correspondingly-numbered stanzas in the version given in the *Gesto Coll.*, p. 1, and in *An t-Oranaiche*. A shorter version with metrical English translation is in *Minstrelsy of the Scottish Highlands*. The second tune in the *Gesto Coll.* (App. p. 25) was contributed by me; the first air and that in the *Minstrelsy of the Scottish Highlands* are very similar to each other, and distinct from mine.—F. T.

Cf. a version of words, with translation, historical note, and music harmonised, in Charles Stewart's *Killin Coll.* The earliest printed version of the tune is probably that noted by Patrick M'Donald before 1760, in Perthshire, and published as No. 88 of his *Highland Vocal Airs* (1781). Miss Tolmie's version seems the oldest, and its cadence more beautiful than others.—L. E. B.

See *The Thistle* and *The Inverness Coll. of Highland Pibrochs*, etc., for other and simpler versions of this fine lament. All the forms of it which I have seen are purely pentatonic, and Miss Tolmie's is an interesting example of the flowing character which may be given to a melody in a gapped scale. The pathos of many Highland laments composed in what appears to be a major key seems to be due to the emotional rise and fall of the melody, like a succession of sighs—to the dying cadences, and to the frequency of the melodic interval of the minor third, ascending or descending.—A. G. G.

98.—FUAIM AN *TAIBH.

(THE SOUND OF THE OCEAN.)

By Mary Macleod.

PENTATONIC.
Mode 1.

SUNG BY MARGARET GILLIES (COTTAR),
BRACADALE, SKYE, 1861.

Grave. *Fine.*

1. 'S mi ri fuaim an   taibh   'S uaig-neach mo ghean. Bha mis' uair   nach b'è sud   m'àbh-aist.

TRANSLATION (abridged).

1. Listening to the sound of the ocean, melancholy is my mood, for not thus has my wont been. 2. But to be hearing a grand, resounding bag-pipe, the strains of which surpassed every other form of music, when touched by the fingers of Patrick. 3. How greatly they err who rely on this world, which so often has changed its perilous pace ! 4. More numerous its courses than drizzling rain coming after dew, in a morning early in May. 5. In my time, no man have I ever seen who has not for a while succumbed to it. 6. Bear this blessing from me to the Hall of Bowls, where the unfortunate find friendly welcome. 7. The abode of abundance, under yonder hillside, where the purpose is, the joy, of my song. 8. Sir Tormod [Norman] beloved, of Olgar's race art thou ; from the beginning, stately thy condition has been.

Mary Macleod (Mairi Nigh 'n Alasdair Ruaidh), born at Rodel, Harris, about the beginning of the first quarter of the seventeenth century, was a gentlewoman who filled the office of nurse in the family of the Chief of Clan Leod, and loved the children so dearly that she composed songs expressive of her devotion to them. But when they began to sicken,

* A loan word from the Norse "haf." The *t* is the ending of the Gaelic article and is prefixed. The spelling "*samh*" in Mackenzie's *Beauties* should be set aside.—G. H.

262

and some of them died, Macleod commanded her to make no more songs, as he believed their effect to be dangerous to those who were the object of such intense feeling. Having disobeyed in this respect, she was punished by being sent away to the Island of Scarba, to the south of Mull, where she was very unhappy. Her poetic faculty, however, did not fail her in this state of seclusion, and she continued to pour forth words of lamentation and of loyalty like the well-known " Luinneag," and the above poem, which may be found (with twenty additional verses under the title " Fuaim an t-shaimh "), in Mackenzie's *Beauties of Gaelic Poetry*. In the course of time Macleod pardoned the exile and sent his galley to convey her home. She died at the age of 105, according to reliable tradition.—F. T.

99.—AN CRÒNAN.

(THE CROON.)

BY MARY MACLEOD.

Mode 4. *a. b.*

SUNG BY MARGARET GILLIES (COTTAR),
BRACADALE, SKYE, 1862.

Lively.

1. An naigh-eachd 'so 'n dé 'S aigh - ear - ach ì!—— Mol - adh do 'n léigh 'thug

mail - eart do m' chéill. Cha ghear - ain mi féin, Na chaill-eadh 's na dh'éug, 'S mo

lean - abh 'na dhéidh comh - shlàn, 'S mo lean - abh 'na dhéidh comh - shlàn !

2. Beannachd do 'n bheul
   Dh 'aithris an sgeul.
   'S fàth mire dhuinn féin,
   'S do 'n chinneadh gu léir,

Do philleadh o 'n éug ;
'S milis an sgeul !
Nis teannaidh mi féin ri crònan.
Nis teannaidh mi féin ri crònan.

TRANSLATION.

1. The news since yesterday, how joyful ! The Physician [*i.e.* God,] be praised, who gave relief to my feelings ! I shall never complain on account of those who are lost, or have died, now my child is to health restored, now my child, etc. 2. Blessing to the mouth that reported the tidings, cause of joy to ourselves, and. to all of the clan ! Thy return from death ! delightful the tale ! Now turn I to singing a croon, now turn I, etc.

The "Croon" was composed by Mary Macleod (*see* p. 262,) on the recovery of the son of the Chief from a dangerous illness. "Did I not forbid thee to make any more songs to my children?" said Macleod. "Ah!" she replied, "this is not a song, but only a 'croon,'" and thus the name was given to it.—F. T.

The opening bars of this tune are very like those of the Cork drinking-song "Beimeedh a gole," in Graves' *Irish Songs and Ballads*—a tune of equal gaiety and abandonment—and there is a similar rhythmical likeness in Dr. Joyce's tune "The Bay and the Grey," No. 146 in his *Old Irish Folk Music*, 1909. As "Beimeedh a gole" is rendered "Let us be drinking," it seems possible that this characteristic opening phrase may have belonged to a "health" sung in the old days. If so, this would give special point to Mary's description of her song as a "croon." There is a tune called "Mary Macleod's Crònan" in the *Inverness Coll. of Highland Pibrochs, Laments, etc.*, but I have not seen this version to compare it with the above.—A. G. G.

See a version of the words (24 stanzas) in Mackenzie's *Beauties, etc.*—L. E. B.

100.—SHIBEAG, SHIBEAG!

(LITTLE SIBELLA.)

PENTATONIC.
Mode 4.

AN EIGG MEMORY,
REVIVED AT BRACADALE MANSE, SKYE, IN 1861.

2. 'S ioma fear a bhios ad dhéidh,
Eadar so is Baile Dhùn-Éidionn,

Cha tugainn do fhear gun spréidh thu,
Euchdag a chùil dualaich!

[By a nurse, 18th century.]

TRANSLATION.

(*Refrain* : Hail to thee, O Sibella, thou gentlewoman!) 1. At thy wedding I shall dance, and be old by that time. (R.) 2. Many a one will woo thee between this [the island of Coll] and Dunedin, but to no one not in possession of flocks and herds would I ever give thy hand, thou charmer of the curling hair!

264

This little "port" or dancing-song is given as an example of a nurse's impromptu adaptation of words to a tune probably already well known, which was sung about the middle of the eighteenth century in the laird's family in the island of Coll, to survive, amidst many changes, in more than one nursery both in Skye and on the mainland. —F. T.

Miss Gilchrist points out that one of the "Jubilee Singers'" hymns, "A Soldier of the Cross" ("I'm going to live with Jesus") is oddly reminiscent of the above, and suggests that a Gaelic marching-tune may have found its way to America and have been adapted by negroes (*cf.* "John Anderson, my jo" and "Johnnie comes marching home" in this connection). Dr. Henderson is of opinion that this is quite possible; he has heard a negro speaking Gaelic, and reminds us that the eighteenth-nineteenth century migrations from the Highlands to America were extensive. I have seen a large MS. collection of Gaelic songs and lore, made, only a few years ago, by an American lady in Cape Breton, where Highland settlers still preserve their language and customs in a most striking way.—L. E. B.

GROUP V.—LAMENTS, LOVE LYRICS, ETC.

101.—CAOIDH LEANNAIN.

(MOURNING FOR ONE BELOVED.)

Mode 2 *a.* (6-note scale.)

SUNG BY MARY ROSS,
FROM KILLMALUAG, SKYE, AT EDINBURGH, 1908.

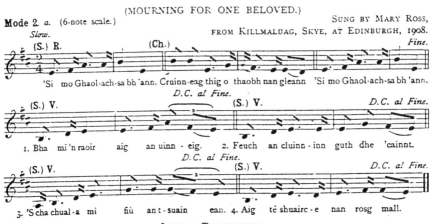

'Si mo Ghaol-ach-sa bh 'ann. Cruinn-eag thig o thaobh nan gleann 'Si mo Ghaol-ach-sa bh 'ann.

1. Bha mi 'n raoir   aig   an uinn - eig.   2. Feuch   an cluinn - inn   guth dhe   'cainnt.

3. 'S cha chual-a mi   fiù   an t - suain   ean. 4. Aig   té shuairc - e   nan rosg   mall.

LITERAL TRANSLATION.

(*Refrain*: It is my darling, *Chorus*: my dear one from the glen-slopes; it is my darling.) 1. Last night I was at the window, (R. and Ch.) 2. to find if I could hear a sound of her voice, 3. and I heard not even a gentle breathing 4. from the meek one of the soft-moving eyes.

The foregoing words are supposed to be uttered by the lover of a girl who has died, unknown to him.—F. T.

102.—CHA DEAN MISE CAR A CHAOIDH.

(MY STRENGTH IS GONE FOR EVERMORE.)

Mode 2 *a. b.* (7-note scale.)
AEOLIAN INFLUENCE.

SUNG BY MARY ROSS,
FROM KILLMALUAG, SKYE, 1899.

R. *Rather slow.*

Cha   dean mis - e   car   a chaoidh,   'N déidh Ann',   an   déidh.   Ann - a!

266

Cha dean mis - e car a chaoidh, an Déidh Ann - a Ràn - uill.

V.

1. Théid mi cuid - e ris na h - eòin, Anns an ath - ar, anns an ath - ar.

Theid mi cuid - e ris na h-eòin, Anns an ath'r a' seòl - adh.

TRANSLATION.

(*Refrain*: My strength is gone for evermore, following Anne, going after Anne, for ever my energy is gone, following Ranald's Anne!) 1. I am going away with the birds into the air, into the air; away I am going with the birds that in the air are sailing. (Ref.)

This tune seems to be a version of "Soldier laddie, highland laddie," and has a similar insistent repeated refrain. The tune has undergone many changes and modifications. Early printed copies are in Playford's *Dancing Master*, 1716 (as "Cockle Shells"), and Walsh's *Compleat Country Dancing Master, circa* 1730, as "The Lass of Livingston." In Gow's *Repository* it appears as "The Original Highland Laddie, or the Quickstep of the gallant 42nd Regiment."—A. G. G.

It is worth adding that Playford's "Cockle Shells" tune reveals a most unexpected link between the air, "The Eagle's Whisper, or Whistle," if put into common time, (see *Journal*, vol. ii. No. 10, p. 34), and the Lowland-Scottish air above quoted.—L. E. B.

103.—FÀILL ILL O-HO-RO.

Mode 3. *a. b.* (7-note scale.)

Moderate.

A MEMORY FROM EIGG, REVIVED AT BRACADALE MANSE, SKYE, IN 1860.

(Ch.)

Fàill ill o - ho - ro, fàill ill ó! Hù ill o - ho - ro, hù ill ó.

Fàill ill éil - e hù ho - ró. O! 'si rùn mo chéill a bh'ann.

(S.)

1. Là dhomh bhi 's a' choill' ud thall, Chunn - ac - as gruag - ach nan rosg mall ;

D.C. al Fine.

Slat - ag 'na làimh 's i cuall - ach mheang. O 'si rùn mo chéill a bh 'ann.

2. Dh 'innsinn dreach mo leannain duit :
   Dà ghruaidh dhearg cho dearg ri subh ;
   Beul gun lochd nach aithris sgeul ;
   O ! 'si rùn mo chéill' a bh 'ann.
                              (Chorus.)

TRANSLATION.

(*Chorus* : Fàill ill, etc. Hu ill, etc. Oh, the joy of my heart was she !) 1. When going over one day to yonder grove, a maiden I met, of soft-moving eyes, holding a twig in her hand while tending kids. Oh, the joy of my heart was she ! (Chorus). 2. Fain would I describe the aspect of her I love : two red cheeks as the raspberries red, and an innocent mouth that repeats no tale. Oh, the joy, etc. (Chorus).

Cf. the air with the version of " An Cluinn thu, Leannain " in Baptie's *Gaelic Songs.* I have noted a very similar tune in Inverness-shire to a song describing a lazy Skye horse and its purchaser's mortification.—L. E. B.

104.—'N UAIR THEID THU DH'AIRIGH-BHUACHAIN.

(WHEN THOU WILT GO TO BUACHAIN SHEILING.)

DORIAN INFLUENCE.

Mode 1. *a. b.* [with ♭3rd].* (7-note scale.)

SUNG BY MRS. M'NEILL,
NEWTON, NORTH UIST, 1871.

* This tune might be allocated to Mode 4. *a. b.* but for the importance of its sixth degree.—A. G. G.

268

The words of this song, heard in early youth, cannot be recalled, but the tune is distinctly remembered. *See* the *Macdonald Collection of Gaelic Poetry* (Inverness, 1911), p. 276, for a text-version. —F. T.

This type of tune, though common in Ireland, is exceedingly rare in Western Highland music. No. 142 in Fraser's *Airs of the Highlands and Isles of Scotland* (ed. 1816) has much the same structure and tonality, but I know of no other Scottish example. —L. E. B.

I feel doubtful whether this tune really belongs to the same modal system as the rest of the airs in this collection. There are two other airs in this number of the Journal showing this rare Dorian influence, to which the same remark applies. These tunes may have come up from the Lowlands, and thus belong to the 7-note system of English folk-songs. —A. G. G.

105.—ORAN AN T-SAIGHDEIR.

(THE SOLDIER'S SONG.)

PENTATONIC.
Mode 3.

SUNG BY PATRICK MACLEOD, (YOUNG SHEPHERD),
AT RUDH AN DÙNAIN, SKYE, 1853.

'N uair bhios mo chàird - ean 'nan cad - al, Air an leab - aidh gu sàmh - ach, 'S ann bhios mis' anns an oidh - che fó an choill' aig mo nàmh - aid. Fo an choill' aig mo nàmh - aid; Feadh mhach-raich-ean còmh-ard; Feadh bheannt - an - an àrd - a, Ag - us fàs - aich - ean ceòth-ach.

TRANSLATION.

When my kindred are slumbering peacefully in bed, I shall be at night in hiding from my enemy. In hiding from my enemy, amid level plains, lofty mountains, and wildernesses enveloped in mist.

This song, of which only one verse can be recollected, was greatly in vogue in Skye, being introduced by a young shepherd, the year before the Crimean war. The words were composed, in his youth, by Major Neil Macleod, R.A., of Waternish, Skye. He died in 1879. For several months every one in our glen sang and hummed this song, whilst at work.—F. T.

Cf. the air with that of the "Raasay Lament," No. 6 in *Songs of the Gael*, and the version of "Crodh Chailein," No. 57 in the *Celtic Lyre*. It belongs to a type of slow three-four major tune which is exceedingly popular in the Western Highlands. For good examples which bear a strong resemblance to the above, and which were all noted in Skye before 1760, *see* Nos. 156, 159, and 160 in Patrick M'Donald's rare *Highland Vocal Airs.*—L. E. B.

APPENDIX.

ACCORDING to traditions surviving in the districts of Moidart, Glen Finnan and Loch Arkaig (Inverness), this song was taboo to men of yore. Colann Gun Cheann, "Body-without-Head," figures in various forms of the legend as a female monster. A version from the part of Inverness above named relates that she was expelled from "Beinn Eadarrainn * (*sic*) in Skye or Harris" for evil doings, and exiled to Cross in the Morar district of Inverness. It is said that she had killed the mother of Ra'ull mac Ailein Oig of Morar's brother, the strongest man in Clan Donald. He was a companion of Iain Garbh mac 'Ille Chaluim of Raasay, whose drowning, attributed to witchcraft, is the subject of Gaelic elegy. Ra'ull (*i.e.* Ronald) mac Ailein Oig's brother gave the monster a weapon, with which she shot off her own head. Her body was able to fly nevertheless, and she fought him all night. In the version which I heard from an old man named Mac Varish, at the head of Loch Arkaig, the monster's habitat was at first at Trost, which the narrator believed to be somewhere in Skye. Mac Varish gave the name "Bealach a Mhoraghain" for "Bealach a Mhòrbheinn." A second verse runs :

> Cùl nam monaidhean, beul nam monaidhean,
> Cùl nam monaidhean, 's aghaidh na maoile ;
> Cùl nam bealaichean, aghaidh nam bealaichean,
> Cùl nam bealaichean, 's aghaidh na maoile.

> (Behind the hills, in front of the hills,
> Behind the hills, in face of the (bare) steep ;
> Behind the (hill-) passes in face of the (hill-) passes,
> Behind the (hill-) passes in face of the (bare) steep.)

The Gaelic words form a sort of mnemonic for the music. Compare the legend with that of Fuath Beinn Edain, or Edair, the giant spectre of the Hill of Howth, near Dublin ; Beinn Edain being the Gaelic name for that hill.

G. H.

* Name probably meaning " Between the two *rinns* or headlands."

INDEX TO GAELIC TITLES.

INDEX TO ENGLISH TITLES.

Also published by Llanerch:

The Complete Collection of Irish Music as noted by George Petrie.

Symbolism of the Celtic Cross by Derek Bryce, with drawings by J. Romilly Allen and others.

The Tombs of the Kings: An Iona Book of the Dead, an account of the kings buried on Iona by John Marsden.

Old Scottish Customs by E. J. Guthrie.

The Romance and Prophecies of Thomas of Erceldoune, edited by James A. H. Murray.

The Culdees of the British Islands, by William Reeves.

Celtic Folk Tales from Armorica, collected by F. M. Luzel, translated by Derek Bryce, with illustrations by Anthony Rhys.

John of Fordun's Chronicle of the Scottish Nation, edited by W. F. Skene.

Folklore of the Scottish Lochs and Springs by James M. Macinlay.

Lives of the Scottish Saints translated by W. Metcalf

(In prepatation - the Gesto Collection of Highland Music, a reprint with the complete Francis Tolmie appendix).

For a complete list of c200 small-press editions and facsimile reprints, write to Llanerch Publishers, Felinfach, Lampeter, Ceredigion, Wales, SA48 8PJ.